# FREE Study Skills DVD Offer

Dear Customer,

Thank you for your purchase from Mometrix! We consider it an honor and a privilege that you have purchased our product and we want to ensure your satisfaction.

As a way of showing our appreciation and to help us better serve you, we have developed a Study Skills DVD that we would like to give you for <u>FREE</u>. This DVD covers our *best practices* for getting ready for your exam, from how to use our study materials to how to best prepare for the day of the test.

All that we ask is that you email us with feedback that would describe your experience so far with our product. Good, bad, or indifferent, we want to know what you think!

To get your FREE Study Skills DVD, email <u>freedvd@mometrix.com</u> with *FREE STUDY SKILLS DVD* in the subject line and the following information in the body of the email:

- The name of the product you purchased.
- Your product rating on a scale of 1-5, with 5 being the highest rating.
- Your feedback. It can be long, short, or anything in between. We just want to know your impressions and experience so far with our product. (Good feedback might include how our study material met your needs and ways we might be able to make it even better. You could highlight features that you found helpful or features that you think we should add.)
- Your full name and shipping address where you would like us to send your free DVD.

If you have any questions or concerns, please don't hesitate to contact me directly.

Thanks again!

Sincerely,

Jay Willis
Vice President
<u>jay.willis@mometrix.com</u>
1-800-673-8175

D1568843

# TOEFL

## iBT

# SECRETS

## Study Guide
### Your Key to Exam Success

Written and edited by the Mometrix English Language Proficiency Test Team

Printed in the United States of America

This paper meets the requirements of ANSI/NISO Z39.48-1992 (Permanence of Paper).

Mometrix offers volume discount pricing to institutions. For more information or a price quote, please contact our sales department at sales@mometrix.com or 888-248-1219.

Mometrix Media LLC is not affiliated with or endorsed by any official testing organization. All organizational and test names are trademarks of their respective owners.

ISBN 13: 978-1-5167-0847-5
ISBN 10: 1516708474

# DEAR FUTURE EXAM SUCCESS STORY

First of all, **THANK YOU** for purchasing Mometrix study materials!

Second, congratulations! You are one of the few determined test-takers who are committed to doing whatever it takes to excel on your exam. **You have come to the right place.** We developed these study materials with one goal in mind: to deliver you the information you need in a format that's concise and easy to use.

In addition to optimizing your guide for the content of the test, we've outlined our recommended steps for breaking down the preparation process into small, attainable goals so you can make sure you stay on track.

We've also analyzed the entire test-taking process, identifying the most common pitfalls and showing how you can overcome them and be ready for any curveball the test throws you.

Standardized testing is one of the biggest obstacles on your road to success, which only increases the importance of doing well in the high-pressure, high-stakes environment of test day. Your results on this test could have a significant impact on your future, and this guide provides the information and practical advice to help you achieve your full potential on test day.

### Your success is our success

**We would love to hear from you!** If you would like to share the story of your exam success or if you have any questions or comments in regard to our products, please contact us at **800-673-8175** or **support@mometrix.com**.

Thanks again for your business and we wish you continued success!

Sincerely,
The Mometrix Test Preparation Team

**Need more help? Check out our flashcards at:**
**http://MometrixFlashcards.com/TOEFL**

# TABLE OF CONTENTS

# Introduction

**Thank you for purchasing this resource!** You have made the choice to prepare yourself for a test that could have a huge impact on your future, and this guide is designed to help you be fully ready for test day. Obviously, it's important to have a solid understanding of the test material, but you also need to be prepared for the unique environment and stressors of the test, so that you can perform to the best of your abilities.

For this purpose, the first section that appears in this guide is the **Secret Keys**. We've devoted countless hours to meticulously researching what works and what doesn't, and we've boiled down our findings to the five most impactful steps you can take to improve your performance on the test. We start at the beginning with study planning and move through the preparation process, all the way to the testing strategies that will help you get the most out of what you know when you're finally sitting in front of the test.

We recommend that you start preparing for your test as far in advance as possible. However, if you've bought this guide as a last-minute study resource and only have a few days before your test, we recommend that you skip over the first two Secret Keys since they address a long-term study plan.

If you struggle with **test anxiety**, we strongly encourage you to check out our recommendations for how you can overcome it. Test anxiety is a formidable foe, but it can be beaten, and we want to make sure you have the tools you need to defeat it.

# Secret Key #1 – Plan Big, Study Small

There's a lot riding on your performance. If you want to ace this test, you're going to need to keep your skills sharp and the material fresh in your mind. You need a plan that lets you review everything you need to know while still fitting in your schedule. We'll break this strategy down into three categories.

## Information Organization

Start with the information you already have: the official test outline. From this, you can make a complete list of all the concepts you need to cover before the test. Organize these concepts into groups that can be studied together, and create a list of any related vocabulary you need to learn so you can brush up on any difficult terms. You'll want to keep this vocabulary list handy once you actually start studying since you may need to add to it along the way.

## Time Management

Once you have your set of study concepts, decide how to spread them out over the time you have left before the test. Break your study plan into small, clear goals so you have a manageable task for each day and know exactly what you're doing. Then just focus on one small step at a time. When you manage your time this way, you don't need to spend hours at a time studying. Studying a small block of content for a short period each day helps you retain information better and avoid stressing over how much you have left to do. You can relax knowing that you have a plan to cover everything in time. In order for this strategy to be effective though, you have to start studying early and stick to your schedule. Avoid the exhaustion and futility that comes from last-minute cramming!

## Study Environment

The environment you study in has a big impact on your learning. Studying in a coffee shop, while probably more enjoyable, is not likely to be as fruitful as studying in a quiet room. It's important to keep distractions to a minimum. You're only planning to study for a short block of time, so make the most of it. Don't pause to check your phone or get up to find a snack. It's also important to **avoid multitasking**. Research has consistently shown that multitasking will make your studying dramatically less effective. Your study area should also be comfortable and well-lit so you don't have the distraction of straining your eyes or sitting on an uncomfortable chair.

The time of day you study is also important. You want to be rested and alert. Don't wait until just before bedtime. Study when you'll be most likely to comprehend and remember. Even better, if you know what time of day your test will be, set that time aside for study. That way your brain will be used to working on that subject at that specific time and you'll have a better chance of recalling information.

Finally, it can be helpful to team up with others who are studying for the same test. Your actual studying should be done in as isolated an environment as possible, but the work of organizing the information and setting up the study plan can be divided up. In between study sessions, you can discuss with your teammates the concepts that you're all studying and quiz each other on the details. Just be sure that your teammates are as serious about the test as you are. If you find that your study time is being replaced with social time, you might need to find a new team.

# Secret Key #2 – Make Your Studying Count

You're devoting a lot of time and effort to preparing for this test, so you want to be absolutely certain it will pay off. This means doing more than just reading the content and hoping you can remember it on test day. It's important to make every minute of study count. There are two main areas you can focus on to make your studying count:

## Retention

It doesn't matter how much time you study if you can't remember the material. You need to make sure you are retaining the concepts. To check your retention of the information you're learning, try recalling it at later times with minimal prompting. Try carrying around flashcards and glance at one or two from time to time or ask a friend who's also studying for the test to quiz you.

To enhance your retention, look for ways to put the information into practice so that you can apply it rather than simply recalling it. If you're using the information in practical ways, it will be much easier to remember. Similarly, it helps to solidify a concept in your mind if you're not only reading it to yourself but also explaining it to someone else. Ask a friend to let you teach them about a concept you're a little shaky on (or speak aloud to an imaginary audience if necessary). As you try to summarize, define, give examples, and answer your friend's questions, you'll understand the concepts better and they will stay with you longer. Finally, step back for a big picture view and ask yourself how each piece of information fits with the whole subject. When you link the different concepts together and see them working together as a whole, it's easier to remember the individual components.

Finally, practice showing your work on any multi-step problems, even if you're just studying. Writing out each step you take to solve a problem will help solidify the process in your mind, and you'll be more likely to remember it during the test.

## Modality

*Modality* simply refers to the means or method by which you study. Choosing a study modality that fits your own individual learning style is crucial. No two people learn best in exactly the same way, so it's important to know your strengths and use them to your advantage.

For example, if you learn best by visualization, focus on visualizing a concept in your mind and draw an image or a diagram. Try color-coding your notes, illustrating them, or creating symbols that will trigger your mind to recall a learned concept. If you learn best by hearing or discussing information, find a study partner who learns the same way or read aloud to yourself. Think about how to put the information in your own words. Imagine that you are giving a lecture on the topic and record yourself so you can listen to it later.

For any learning style, flashcards can be helpful. Organize the information so you can take advantage of spare moments to review. Underline key words or phrases. Use different colors for different categories. Mnemonic devices (such as creating a short list in which every item starts with the same letter) can also help with retention. Find what works best for you and use it to store the information in your mind most effectively and easily.

# Secret Key #3 – Practice the Right Way

Your success on test day depends not only on how many hours you put into preparing, but also on whether you prepared the right way. It's good to check along the way to see if your studying is paying off. One of the most effective ways to do this is by taking practice tests to evaluate your progress. Practice tests are useful because they show exactly where you need to improve. Every time you take a practice test, pay special attention to these three groups of questions:

- The questions you got wrong
- The questions you had to guess on, even if you guessed right
- The questions you found difficult or slow to work through

This will show you exactly what your weak areas are, and where you need to devote more study time. Ask yourself why each of these questions gave you trouble. Was it because you didn't understand the material? Was it because you didn't remember the vocabulary? Do you need more repetitions on this type of question to build speed and confidence? Dig into those questions and figure out how you can strengthen your weak areas as you go back to review the material.

Additionally, many practice tests have a section explaining the answer choices. It can be tempting to read the explanation and think that you now have a good understanding of the concept. However, an explanation likely only covers part of the question's broader context. Even if the explanation makes sense, **go back and investigate** every concept related to the question until you're positive you have a thorough understanding.

As you go along, keep in mind that the practice test is just that: practice. Memorizing these questions and answers will not be very helpful on the actual test because it is unlikely to have any of the same exact questions. If you only know the right answers to the sample questions, you won't be prepared for the real thing. **Study the concepts** until you understand them fully, and then you'll be able to answer any question that shows up on the test.

It's important to wait on the practice tests until you're ready. If you take a test on your first day of study, you may be overwhelmed by the amount of material covered and how much you need to learn. Work up to it gradually.

On test day, you'll need to be prepared for answering questions, managing your time, and using the test-taking strategies you've learned. It's a lot to balance, like a mental marathon that will have a big impact on your future. Like training for a marathon, you'll need to start slowly and work your way up. When test day arrives, you'll be ready.

Start with the strategies you've read in the first two Secret Keys—plan your course and study in the way that works best for you. If you have time, consider using multiple study resources to get different approaches to the same concepts. It can be helpful to see difficult concepts from more than one angle. Then find a good source for practice tests. Many times, the test website will suggest potential study resources or provide sample tests.

# Practice Test Strategy

If you're able to find at least three practice tests, we recommend this strategy:

## UNTIMED AND OPEN-BOOK PRACTICE

Take the first test with no time constraints and with your notes and study guide handy. Take your time and focus on applying the strategies you've learned.

## TIMED AND OPEN-BOOK PRACTICE

Take the second practice test open-book as well, but set a timer and practice pacing yourself to finish in time.

## TIMED AND CLOSED-BOOK PRACTICE

Take any other practice tests as if it were test day. Set a timer and put away your study materials. Sit at a table or desk in a quiet room, imagine yourself at the testing center, and answer questions as quickly and accurately as possible.

Keep repeating timed and closed-book tests on a regular basis until you run out of practice tests or it's time for the actual test. Your mind will be ready for the schedule and stress of test day, and you'll be able to focus on recalling the material you've learned.

# Secret Key #4 – Pace Yourself

Once you're fully prepared for the material on the test, your biggest challenge on test day will be managing your time. Just knowing that the clock is ticking can make you panic even if you have plenty of time left. Work on pacing yourself so you can build confidence against the time constraints of the exam. Pacing is a difficult skill to master, especially in a high-pressure environment, so **practice is vital**.

Set time expectations for your pace based on how much time is available. For example, if a section has 60 questions and the time limit is 30 minutes, you know you have to average 30 seconds or less per question in order to answer them all. Although 30 seconds is the hard limit, set 25 seconds per question as your goal, so you reserve extra time to spend on harder questions. When you budget extra time for the harder questions, you no longer have any reason to stress when those questions take longer to answer.

Don't let this time expectation distract you from working through the test at a calm, steady pace, but keep it in mind so you don't spend too much time on any one question. Recognize that taking extra time on one question you don't understand may keep you from answering two that you do understand later in the test. If your time limit for a question is up and you're still not sure of the answer, mark it and move on, and come back to it later if the time and the test format allow. If the testing format doesn't allow you to return to earlier questions, just make an educated guess; then put it out of your mind and move on.

On the easier questions, be careful not to rush. It may seem wise to hurry through them so you have more time for the challenging ones, but it's not worth missing one if you know the concept and just didn't take the time to read the question fully. Work efficiently but make sure you understand the question and have looked at all of the answer choices, since more than one may seem right at first.

Even if you're paying attention to the time, you may find yourself a little behind at some point. You should speed up to get back on track, but do so wisely. Don't panic; just take a few seconds less on each question until you're caught up. Don't guess without thinking, but do look through the answer choices and eliminate any you know are wrong. If you can get down to two choices, it is often worthwhile to guess from those. Once you've chosen an answer, move on and don't dwell on any that you skipped or had to hurry through. If a question was taking too long, chances are it was one of the harder ones, so you weren't as likely to get it right anyway.

On the other hand, if you find yourself getting ahead of schedule, it may be beneficial to slow down a little. The more quickly you work, the more likely you are to make a careless mistake that will affect your score. You've budgeted time for each question, so don't be afraid to spend that time. Practice an efficient but careful pace to get the most out of the time you have.

# Secret Key #5 – Have a Plan for Guessing

When you're taking the test, you may find yourself stuck on a question. Some of the answer choices seem better than others, but you don't see the one answer choice that is obviously correct. What do you do?

The scenario described above is very common, yet most test takers have not effectively prepared for it. Developing and practicing a plan for guessing may be one of the single most effective uses of your time as you get ready for the exam.

In developing your plan for guessing, there are three questions to address:

- When should you start the guessing process?
- How should you narrow down the choices?
- Which answer should you choose?

## When to Start the Guessing Process

Unless your plan for guessing is to select C every time (which, despite its merits, is not what we recommend), you need to leave yourself enough time to apply your answer elimination strategies. Since you have a limited amount of time for each question, that means that if you're going to give yourself the best shot at guessing correctly, you have to decide quickly whether or not you will guess.

Of course, the best-case scenario is that you don't have to guess at all, so first, see if you can answer the question based on your knowledge of the subject and basic reasoning skills. Focus on the key words in the question and try to jog your memory of related topics. Give yourself a chance to bring the knowledge to mind, but once you realize that you don't have (or you can't access) the knowledge you need to answer the question, it's time to start the guessing process.

It's almost always better to start the guessing process too early than too late. It only takes a few seconds to remember something and answer the question from knowledge. Carefully eliminating wrong answer choices takes longer. Plus, going through the process of eliminating answer choices can actually help jog your memory.

**Summary**: Start the guessing process as soon as you decide that you can't answer the question based on your knowledge.

# How to Narrow Down the Choices

The next chapter in this book (**Test-Taking Strategies**) includes a wide range of strategies for how to approach questions and how to look for answer choices to eliminate. You will definitely want to read those carefully, practice them, and figure out which ones work best for you. Here though, we're going to address a mindset rather than a particular strategy.

Your chances of guessing an answer correctly depend on how many options you are choosing from.

| How many choices you have | How likely you are to guess correctly |
|---|---|
| 5 | 20% |
| 4 | 25% |
| 3 | 33% |
| 2 | 50% |
| 1 | 100% |

You can see from this chart just how valuable it is to be able to eliminate incorrect answers and make an educated guess, but there are two things that many test takers do that cause them to miss out on the benefits of guessing:

- Accidentally eliminating the correct answer
- Selecting an answer based on an impression

We'll look at the first one here, and the second one in the next section.

To avoid accidentally eliminating the correct answer, we recommend a thought exercise called **the $5 challenge**. In this challenge, you only eliminate an answer choice from contention if you are willing to bet $5 on it being wrong. Why $5? Five dollars is a small but not insignificant amount of money. It's an amount you could afford to lose but wouldn't want to throw away. And while losing $5 once might not hurt too much, doing it twenty times will set you back $100. In the same way, each small decision you make—eliminating a choice here, guessing on a question there—won't by itself impact your score very much, but when you put them all together, they can make a big difference. By holding each answer choice elimination decision to a higher standard, you can reduce the risk of accidentally eliminating the correct answer.

The $5 challenge can also be applied in a positive sense: If you are willing to bet $5 that an answer choice *is* correct, go ahead and mark it as correct.

**Summary**: Only eliminate an answer choice if you are willing to bet $5 that it is wrong.

# Which Answer to Choose

You're taking the test. You've run into a hard question and decided you'll have to guess. You've eliminated all the answer choices you're willing to bet $5 on. Now you have to pick an answer. Why do we even need to talk about this? Why can't you just pick whichever one you feel like when the time comes?

The answer to these questions is that if you don't come into the test with a plan, you'll rely on your impression to select an answer choice, and if you do that, you risk falling into a trap. The test writers know that everyone who takes their test will be guessing on some of the questions, so they intentionally write wrong answer choices to seem plausible. You still have to pick an answer though, and if the wrong answer choices are designed to look right, how can you ever be sure that you're not falling for their trap? The best solution we've found to this dilemma is to take the decision out of your hands entirely. Here is the process we recommend:

**Once you've eliminated any choices that you are confident (willing to bet $5) are wrong, select the first remaining choice as your answer.**

Whether you choose to select the first remaining choice, the second, or the last, the important thing is that you use some preselected standard. Using this approach guarantees that you will not be enticed into selecting an answer choice that looks right, because you are not basing your decision on how the answer choices look.

This is not meant to make you question your knowledge. Instead, it is to help you recognize the difference between your knowledge and your impressions. There's a huge difference between thinking an answer is right because of what you know, and thinking an answer is right because it looks or sounds like it should be right.

**Summary**: To ensure that your selection is appropriately random, make a predetermined selection from among all answer choices you have not eliminated.

9

# Test-Taking Strategies

This section contains a list of test-taking strategies that you may find helpful as you work through the test. By taking what you know and applying logical thought, you can maximize your chances of answering any question correctly!

It is very important to realize that every question is different and every person is different: no single strategy will work on every question, and no single strategy will work for every person. That's why we've included all of them here, so you can try them out and determine which ones work best for different types of questions and which ones work best for you.

## Question Strategies

### READ CAREFULLY

Read the question and answer choices carefully. Don't miss the question because you misread the terms. You have plenty of time to read each question thoroughly and make sure you understand what is being asked. Yet a happy medium must be attained, so don't waste too much time. You must read carefully, but efficiently.

### CONTEXTUAL CLUES

Look for contextual clues. If the question includes a word you are not familiar with, look at the immediate context for some indication of what the word might mean. Contextual clues can often give you all the information you need to decipher the meaning of an unfamiliar word. Even if you can't determine the meaning, you may be able to narrow down the possibilities enough to make a solid guess at the answer to the question.

### PREFIXES

If you're having trouble with a word in the question or answer choices, try dissecting it. Take advantage of every clue that the word might include. Prefixes and suffixes can be a huge help. Usually they allow you to determine a basic meaning. Pre- means before, post- means after, pro - is positive, de- is negative. From prefixes and suffixes, you can get an idea of the general meaning of the word and try to put it into context.

### HEDGE WORDS

Watch out for critical hedge words, such as *likely, may, can, sometimes, often, almost, mostly, usually, generally, rarely*, and *sometimes*. Question writers insert these hedge phrases to cover every possibility. Often an answer choice will be wrong simply because it leaves no room for exception. Be on guard for answer choices that have definitive words such as *exactly* and *always*.

### SWITCHBACK WORDS

Stay alert for *switchbacks*. These are the words and phrases frequently used to alert you to shifts in thought. The most common switchback words are *but, although*, and *however*. Others include *nevertheless, on the other hand, even though, while, in spite of, despite, regardless of*. Switchback words are important to catch because they can change the direction of the question or an answer choice.

## FACE VALUE

When in doubt, use common sense. Accept the situation in the problem at face value. Don't read too much into it. These problems will not require you to make wild assumptions. If you have to go beyond creativity and warp time or space in order to have an answer choice fit the question, then you should move on and consider the other answer choices. These are normal problems rooted in reality. The applicable relationship or explanation may not be readily apparent, but it is there for you to figure out. Use your common sense to interpret anything that isn't clear.

# Answer Choice Strategies

## ANSWER SELECTION

The most thorough way to pick an answer choice is to identify and eliminate wrong answers until only one is left, then confirm it is the correct answer. Sometimes an answer choice may immediately seem right, but be careful. The test writers will usually put more than one reasonable answer choice on each question, so take a second to read all of them and make sure that the other choices are not equally obvious. As long as you have time left, it is better to read every answer choice than to pick the first one that looks right without checking the others.

## ANSWER CHOICE FAMILIES

An answer choice family consists of two (in rare cases, three) answer choices that are very similar in construction and cannot all be true at the same time. If you see two answer choices that are direct opposites or parallels, one of them is usually the correct answer. For instance, if one answer choice says that quantity $x$ increases and another either says that quantity $x$ decreases (opposite) or says that quantity $y$ increases (parallel), then those answer choices would fall into the same family. An answer choice that doesn't match the construction of the answer choice family is more likely to be incorrect. Most questions will not have answer choice families, but when they do appear, you should be prepared to recognize them.

## ELIMINATE ANSWERS

Eliminate answer choices as soon as you realize they are wrong, but make sure you consider all possibilities. If you are eliminating answer choices and realize that the last one you are left with is also wrong, don't panic. Start over and consider each choice again. There may be something you missed the first time that you will realize on the second pass.

## AVOID FACT TRAPS

Don't be distracted by an answer choice that is factually true but doesn't answer the question. You are looking for the choice that answers the question. Stay focused on what the question is asking for so you don't accidentally pick an answer that is true but incorrect. Always go back to the question and make sure the answer choice you've selected actually answers the question and is not merely a true statement.

## EXTREME STATEMENTS

In general, you should avoid answers that put forth extreme actions as standard practice or proclaim controversial ideas as established fact. An answer choice that states the "process should be used in certain situations, if..." is much more likely to be correct than one that states the "process should be discontinued completely." The first is a calm rational statement and doesn't even make a definitive, uncompromising stance, using a hedge word *if* to provide wiggle room, whereas the second choice is a radical idea and far more extreme.

11

## BENCHMARK

As you read through the answer choices and you come across one that seems to answer the question well, mentally select that answer choice. This is not your final answer, but it's the one that will help you evaluate the other answer choices. The one that you selected is your benchmark or standard for judging each of the other answer choices. Every other answer choice must be compared to your benchmark. That choice is correct until proven otherwise by another answer choice beating it. If you find a better answer, then that one becomes your new benchmark. Once you've decided that no other choice answers the question as well as your benchmark, you have your final answer.

## PREDICT THE ANSWER

Before you even start looking at the answer choices, it is often best to try to predict the answer. When you come up with the answer on your own, it is easier to avoid distractions and traps because you will know exactly what to look for. The right answer choice is unlikely to be word-for-word what you came up with, but it should be a close match. Even if you are confident that you have the right answer, you should still take the time to read each option before moving on.

# General Strategies

## TOUGH QUESTIONS

If you are stumped on a problem or it appears too hard or too difficult, don't waste time. Move on! Remember though, if you can quickly check for obviously incorrect answer choices, your chances of guessing correctly are greatly improved. Before you completely give up, at least try to knock out a couple of possible answers. Eliminate what you can and then guess at the remaining answer choices before moving on.

## CHECK YOUR WORK

Since you will probably not know every term listed and the answer to every question, it is important that you get credit for the ones that you do know. Don't miss any questions through careless mistakes. If at all possible, try to take a second to look back over your answer selection and make sure you've selected the correct answer choice and haven't made a costly careless mistake (such as marking an answer choice that you didn't mean to mark). This quick double check should more than pay for itself in caught mistakes for the time it costs.

## PACE YOURSELF

It's easy to be overwhelmed when you're looking at a page full of questions; your mind is confused and full of random thoughts, and the clock is ticking down faster than you would like. Calm down and maintain the pace that you have set for yourself. Especially as you get down to the last few minutes of the test, don't let the small numbers on the clock make you panic. As long as you are on track by monitoring your pace, you are guaranteed to have time for each question.

## DON'T RUSH

It is very easy to make errors when you are in a hurry. Maintaining a fast pace in answering questions is pointless if it makes you miss questions that you would have gotten right otherwise. Test writers like to include distracting information and wrong answers that seem right. Taking a little extra time to avoid careless mistakes can make all the difference in your test score. Find a pace that allows you to be confident in the answers that you select.

## KEEP MOVING

Panicking will not help you pass the test, so do your best to stay calm and keep moving. Taking deep breaths and going through the answer elimination steps you practiced can help to break through a stress barrier and keep your pace.

# Final Notes

The combination of a solid foundation of content knowledge and the confidence that comes from practicing your plan for applying that knowledge is the key to maximizing your performance on test day. As your foundation of content knowledge is built up and strengthened, you'll find that the strategies included in this chapter become more and more effective in helping you quickly sift through the distractions and traps of the test to isolate the correct answer.

Now it's time to move on to the test content chapters of this book, but be sure to keep your goal in mind. As you read, think about how you will be able to apply this information on the test. If you've already seen sample questions for the test and you have an idea of the question format and style, try to come up with questions of your own that you can answer based on what you're reading. This will give you valuable practice applying your knowledge in the same ways you can expect to on test day.

**Good luck and good studying!**

# Reading

The Reading section of the TOEFL consists of a total of 30-40 questions which will last from 54-72 minutes.

There are three to four passages, which will each be followed by ten questions each.

## Tips for the Reading Section

The reading section requires you to demonstrate your ability to find information, use basic comprehension, and read to learn.

### TIP 1: READING TO FIND INFORMATION

When reading to find specific ideas, it is important to be able to **scan** or **skim** a text for a specific phrase or context. To improve your reading speed and ability to scan a text, find passages that discuss a specific topic and practice looking for main ideas quickly without taking the time to read every word or sentence.

### TIP 2: BASIC COMPREHENSION

When reading for basic comprehension of a passage, you will likely be asked to identify **themes, main ideas, and vocabulary** in context. These pieces of information are most likely to be found in the first sentence of the paragraph and in introductory or conclusion paragraphs. Spend some time reading through paragraphs and short stories looking for key information.

### TIP 3: READING TO LEARN

When reading to learn, one must be aware of **organization** and **presentation** of information within a passage. As you read through passages, try to identify the point of a passage, as well as whether it is speaking in an informative or persuasive manner. Keep track of important details, as some questions may require you to insert sentences that fit best in a passage. In these questions, there may be more than one answer that is technically correct, but only one that is truly the best fit.

# Reading Comprehension Skills

This section is organized to introduce you to the passages that you will find on your exam. We cover the different types of passages from narrative to persuasive. Then, we move to the reason that a passage is written. As you may know, some texts are written to persuade. Other passages want to inform.

The writing devices used by writers are important to understand as you practice reading passages. The other parts of a passage we focus on are main ideas, supporting details, and themes. Then, we review making inferences and drawing conclusions. With this step-by-step guide, you will move to a higher score on your test.

Careful reading and thinking about a passage are important in every part of life. Work with this information by reading books, magazines, or newspapers. When you read carefully, you can use this information for other passages. With practice you will strengthen your skills for the future.

## TYPES OF PASSAGES

A **narrative** passage is a story that can be fiction or nonfiction (i.e., false or true). To be a narrative, the passage must have a few things. First, the text must have a plot (i.e., an order of events). Some narratives are written in a clear order, but this is not necessary. If the narrative is good, then you will find these events interesting. Second, a narrative has characters. These characters can be people, animals, or even lifeless items. As long as they play in the plot, they are characters. Third, a narrative passage often has figurative language. This is a tool that authors use to stir the imagination of readers with comparisons or comments. For example, a metaphor is a comparison between two things without using the words *like* or *as*. *He stood like a king* is not an example of a metaphor. *The moon was a frosty snowball* is an example of a metaphor. In reality, this is not true. Yet, the comparison creates a vivid mental image for readers.

An **expository** passage aims to inform or teach readers. The passage is nonfiction and usually centers around an easily explained topic. Often, an expository passage has helpful organizing words such as *first, next, for example*, and *therefore*. These words let readers know where they are in the passage. While expository passages don't need to have difficult vocabulary and fancy writing, they may be improved by them. Yet this can make it difficult to pay attention to an expository passage. Expository passages are not always on topics you will find interesting. Also, writers focus more on clarity and precision than with keeping the reader's interest. By careful reading, you will establish a good habit of focus when you read an expository passage.

A **technical** passage is written to describe a complicated thing or action. Technical writing is common in medical and technology fields. In those fields, ideas of mathematics, science, and engineering need to be explained simply and clearly. A technical passage usually proceeds in a step-by-step order to help with understanding the passage. Technical passages often have clear headings and subheadings. These headings act like the organizing words in an expository passage: they let readers know where they are in a passage. Also, you will find that these passages divide sections by numbers or letters. Many technical passages look more like an outline than the paragraphs that you are reading right now. Depending on the audience, the amount of difficult vocabulary will change in a technical passage. Some technical passages try to stay away from language that readers will have to look up. However, some difficult vocabulary has to be used for writers to share their message.

A **persuasive** passage is written to change the minds of readers so that they agree with the author. The purpose of the passage may be very clear or very difficult to find. A persuasive passage wants to make an acceptable argument and win the trust of the reader. In some cases, a persuasive passage will be similar to an informative passage. Both passages make an argument and offer supporting details. However, a persuasive passage is more likely to appeal to the reader's feelings and make arguments based on opinions. Persuasive passages may not describe other points of view. So, when they do show other points of view, they may show favoritism to one side.

Persuasive passages will focus on one **main argument** and make many **minor arguments** (i.e., arguments that help the main argument) along the way. If you are going to accept the main argument, then you need to accept the minor arguments. So, the main argument will only be as strong as the minor arguments. These arguments should be rooted in fact and experience, not opinions. The best persuasive passages give enough supporting detail to back up arguments without confusing readers. Remember that a fact must be open to independent verification (i.e., the fact must be something that can be backed up by someone else). Also, statistics (i.e., data or figures are collected for study) are helpful only when they look at other choices. For example, a statistic on the number of bicycles sold would only be useful if it was taken over a limited time period and in a specific area. Good readers are careful with statistics because statistics can show what the author wants us to see. Or, they can hide what the author doesn't want to show. The writers of your test know that their passages will be met by questioning readers. So, your skill at questioning what you read will be a help in your exam.

**Opinions** come from how we feel and what we think. Persuasive writers often try to appeal to the emotions (i.e., use or influence someone's feelings) of readers to make their arguments. You should always ask questions about this approach. You should ask questions because an author can pull you into accepting something that you don't want to accept. Sometimes these appeals can be used fairly. For example, some subjects cannot be totally addressed without an appeal to a reader's feelings. Think about an article on drunk driving. Some examples in the article will alarm or sadden readers because of the terrible outcome.

On the other hand, appeals to feelings are unacceptable when they try to **mislead** readers. For example, a presidential candidate (i.e., someone running for president) says that he/she cares about the country. The candidate pushes you to make a connection. You care about the country as well and have positive feelings toward it. The candidate wants you to connect your positive feelings about the country with your thoughts about him or her. If you make more connections with the candidate, then you are likely to vote for him or her. Also, the person running for president hints that other candidates do not care about the country.

Another common and unacceptable appeal to feelings is the use of **loaded language**. Calling a religious person a *fanatic* or a person interested in the environment a *tree hugger* are examples of loaded language.

> **Review Video: <u>Appeal to Emotion</u>**
> Visit mometrix.com/academy and enter code: 163442

## ORGANIZATION OF THE PASSAGE

The way a passage is organized can help readers to understand the author's purpose and conclusions. There are many ways to organize a passage, and each one has an important use.

Some nonfiction texts are organized to present a **problem** followed by a **solution**. For this type of passage, the problem is explained before the solution is given. When the problem is well known, the solution may be given in a few sentences at the beginning. Other passages may focus on the solution, and the problem will be talked about a few times. Some passages will outline many solutions to a problem. This will leave you to choose among the possible solutions. If authors have loyalty to one solution, they may not describe some of the other solutions. Be careful with the author's plan when reading a problem-solution passage. When you know the author's point of view, you can make a better judgment of the solution.

Sometimes authors will organize information clearly for you to follow and locate the information. However, this is not always the case with passages in an exam. Two common ways to order a passage are cause and effect and chronological order. When using **chronological order** (i.e., a plan that moves in order from the first step to the last), the author gives information in the order that the event happened. For example, biographies are written in chronological order. The person's birth and childhood are first. Their adult life is next. The events leading up to the person's death are last.

In **cause and effect**, an author shows one thing that makes something else happen. For example, if one were to go to bed very late and wake up very early, he/she would be tired in the morning. The cause is lack of sleep, with the effect of being tired the next day.

Finding the cause-and-effect relationships in a passage can be tricky. Often, these relationships come with certain words or terms. When authors use words like *because, since, in order*, and *so*, they are describing a cause and effect relationship. Think about the sentence: *He called her because he needed the homework*. This is a simple causal relationship. The cause was his need for the homework, and the effect was his phone call. However, not all cause and effect relationships are marked like this. Think about the sentences: *He called her. He needed the homework*. When the cause-and-effect relationship does not come with a keyword, the relationship can be known by asking why. For example, He called her: *why?* The answer is in the next sentence: He needed the homework.

When authors try to change the minds of readers, they may use cause-and-effect relationships. However, these relationships should not always be taken at face value. To read a persuasive essay well, you need to judge the cause-and-effect relationships. For example, imagine an author wrote the following: *The parking deck has not been making money because people want to ride their bikes*. The relationship is clear: the cause is that people want to ride their bikes. The effect is that the parking deck has not been making money. However, you should look at this argument again. Maybe there are other reasons that the parking deck was not a success: a bad economy, too many costs, etc.

Many passages follow the **compare-and-contrast** model. In this model, the similarities and differences between two ideas or things are reviewed. A review of the similarities between ideas is called comparison. In a perfect comparison, the author shows ideas or things in the same way. If authors want to show the similarities between football and baseball, they can list the equipment and rules for each game. Think about the similarities as they appear in the passage and take note of any differences.

Careful thinking about ideas and conclusions can seem like a difficult task. You can make this task easy by understanding the basic parts of ideas and writing skills. Looking at the way that ideas link to others is a good way to begin. Sometimes authors will write about two opposing ideas. Other times, an author will support a topic, and another author will argue against the topic. The review of these rival ideas is known as **contrast**. In contrast, all ideas should be presented clearly. If the author does favor a side, you need to read carefully to find how the author shows or hides this favoritism. Also, as you read the passage, you should write out how one side views the other.

## PURPOSES FOR WRITING

To be a careful reader, pay attention to the author's **position** and purpose. Even passages that seem fair and equal--like textbooks--have a position or bias (i.e., the author is unfair or inaccurate with opposing ideas). Readers need to take these positions into account when considering the author's message. Authors who appeal to feelings or favor one side of an argument make their position clear. Authors' positions may be found in what they write and in what they don't write. Normally, you would want to review other passages on the same topic to understand the author's position. However, you are in the middle of an exam. So, look for language and arguments that show a position.

**Review Video: Author's Position**
Visit mometrix.com/academy and enter code: 827954

Sometimes, finding the **purpose** of an author is easier than finding his or her position. In most cases, the author has no interest in hiding his or her purpose. A passage for *entertainment* will be written to please readers. Most stories are written to entertain. However, they can inform or persuade. *Informative* texts are easy to recognize. The most difficult purpose of a text to determine is *persuasion*. In persuasion, the author wants to make the purpose hard to find. When you learn that the author wants to persuade, you should be skeptical of the argument. Persuasive passages try to establish an entertaining tone and hope to amuse you into agreement. On the other hand, an informative tone may be used to seem fair and equal to all sides.

An author's purpose is clear often in the **organization** of the text (such as section headings in bold font points for an informative passage). However, you may not have this organization in your passages. So, if authors make their main idea clear from the beginning, then their likely purpose is to *inform*. If the author makes a main argument and gives minor arguments for support, then the purpose is probably to *persuade*. If the author tells a story, then his or her purpose is most likely to *entertain*. If the author wants to gain your attention more than to persuade or inform, then his or her purpose is most likely to entertain. You must judge authors by how well they achieve their purpose. In other words, think about the type of passage (technical, persuasive, etc.) that the author has written and whether the author has followed the demands of the passage type.

**Review Video: Purpose of an Author**
Visit mometrix.com/academy and enter code: 497555

The author's purpose will influence his or her writing approach and the reader's reaction. In a **persuasive essay**, the author wants to prove something to readers. There are several important marks of persuasive writing. Opinion given as fact is one mark. When authors try to persuade readers, they give their opinions as if they were facts. Readers must be on guard for statements that sound like facts but cannot be tested. Another mark of persuasive writing is the appeal to feelings. An author will try to play with the feelings of readers by appealing to their ideas of what is right and wrong. When an author uses strong language to excite the reader's feelings, then the author may want to persuade. Many times, a persuasive passage will give an unfair explanation of other sides, or simply not show the other sides.

An **informative passage** is written to teach readers. Informative passages are almost always nonfiction. The purpose of an informative passage is to share information in the clearest way. In an informative passage, you may have a *thesis statement* (an argument on the topic of a passage that is later proven). A thesis statement is a sentence that normally comes at the end of the first paragraph. Authors of informative passages are likely to place more importance on clarity. Informative

19

passages do not normally appeal to the feelings. They often contain facts and figures, and almost never include the author's opinion. However, you should know that there can be a bias in the facts. Sometimes, a persuasive passage can be like an informative passage. This is true when authors give their ideas as if they were facts.

**Entertainment passages** describe real or imagined people, places, and events. Entertainment passages are often stories or poems. So, figurative language is a common part of these passages. Often, an entertainment passage appeals to the imagination and feelings. Authors may persuade or inform in an entertainment passage. Or, an entertainment passage may cause readers to think differently about a subject.

When authors want to **share feelings,** they may use strong language. Authors may share feelings about a moment of great pain or happiness. Other times, authors will try to persuade readers by sharing feelings. Some phrases like *I felt* and *I sense* hint that the author is sharing feelings. Authors may share stories of deep pain or great joy. You must not be influenced by these stories. You need to keep some distance to judge the author's argument.

Almost all writing is descriptive. In one way or another, authors try to describe events, ideas, or people. But some texts are concerned only with **description**. A descriptive passage focuses on a single subject and seeks to explain the subject clearly. Descriptive passages contain many adjectives and adverbs (words that give a complete picture for you to imagine). Normally, a descriptive passage is informative. Yet, the passage may be persuasive or entertaining.

## WRITING DEVICES

Authors will use different writing devices to make their message clear for readers. One of those devices is comparison and contrast. As mentioned above, when authors show how two things are alike, they are **comparing** them. When authors describe how two things are different, they are **contrasting** them. The compare and contrast passage is a common part of nonfiction. Comparisons are known by certain words or phrases: *both, same, like, too,* and *as well.* Contrasts may have words or phrases like *but, however, on the other hand, instead,* and *yet.* Of course, comparisons and contrasts may be understood without using those words or phrases. A single sentence may compare and contrast. Think about the sentence *Brian and Sheila love ice cream, but Brian loves vanilla and Sheila loves strawberry.* In one sentence, the author has described both a similarity (love of ice cream) and a difference (favorite flavor).

> **Review Video: Compare and Contrast**
> Visit mometrix.com/academy and enter code: 798319

Another regular writing device is **cause and effect**. A cause is an act or event that makes something happen. An effect is what comes from the cause. A cause and effect relationship is not always easy to find. Several words and phrases can be used to show causes: *since, because,* and *due to.* Words and phrases that show effects include *consequently, therefore, this lead(s) to, as a result.* For example, a cause and effect sentence is: *Because the sky was clear, Ron did not bring an umbrella.* The cause is the clear sky, and the effect is that Ron did not bring an umbrella. Readers may find that the cause and effect relationship is not clear. For example, *He was late and missed the meeting.* This does not have any words that show cause or effect. Yet, the sentence still has a cause (he was late) and an effect (he missed the meeting).

Remember the chance for a **single cause** to have many effects. For example, a single-cause sentence is: *Because you left your homework on the table, your dog eats the homework.* The single cause of leaving homework on the table can have many effects: (1) You fail your homework. (2) Your parents do not let you see your friends. (3) You miss out on the new movie. (4) You miss holding the hand of an important person.

Also, a **single effect** can have many causes. For example, a single-effect sentence is: *Alan has a fever*. This fever can have multiple causes: 1) An unexpected cold front came through the area. (2) Alan forgot to take his multi-vitamin.

An effect can also become the cause of another effect. This is known as a **cause and effect chain**. For example: *As a result of her hatred for not doing work, Lynn got ready for her exam*. This led to her passing her test with high marks. Hence, her resume was accepted, and her application was also accepted.

Often, authors use analogies to add meaning to their passages. An **analogy** is a comparison of two things. The words in the analogy are connected by a relationship. Look at this analogy: *moo is to cow as quack is to duck*. This analogy compares the sound that a cow makes with the sound that a duck makes. What could you do if the word *quack* was not given? Well, you could finish the analogy if you know the connection between *moo* and *cow*. Relationships for analogies include synonyms, antonyms, part to whole, definition, and actor to action.

**Point of view** has an important influence on a passage. A passage's point of view is how the author or a character sees or thinks about things. A point of view influences the events of a passage, the meetings among characters, and the ending to the story. For example, two characters watch a child ride a bike. Character one watches outside. Character two watches from inside a house. Both see the same event, yet they are around different noises, sights, and smells. Character one may see different things that happen outside that character two cannot see from inside. Also, point of view can be influenced by past events and beliefs. For example, if character one loves bikes, then she will remember how proud she is of the child. If character two is afraid of riding bikes, then he may not remember the event or may fear for the child's safety.

In fiction, the two main points of view are **first person** and **third person**. The *narrator* is the person who tells a story's events. The *protagonist* is the main character of a story. If the narrator is the protagonist in a story, then the story is written in first-person. In first person, the author writes from the view of *I*. Third-person point of view is the most common among stories. With third person, authors refer to each character by using *he* or *she* and the narrator is not involved in the story. In third-person omniscient, the narrator is not a character in the story and tells the story of all of the characters at the same time.

**Review Video: Point of View**
Visit mometrix.com/academy and enter code: 383336

**Transitional words** and phrases are devices that guide readers through a passage. You may know the common transitions, though you may not have thought about how they are used. Some transitional phrases (*after, before, during, in the middle of*) give information about time. Some hint that an example is about to be given (*for example, in fact, for instance*). Writers use transitions to compare (*also, likewise*) and contrast (*however, but, yet*). Transitional words and phrases can point to addition (*and, also, furthermore, moreover*) and understood relationships (*if, then, therefore, as a result, since*). Finally, transitional words and phrases can separate the chronological steps (*first, second, last*).

**Review Video: Transitional Words and Phrases**
Visit mometrix.com/academy and enter code: 197796

## UNDERSTANDING A PASSAGE

One of the most important skills in reading comprehension is finding **topics** and **main ideas.** There is a small difference between these two. The topic is the *subject* of a passage (what the passage is all about). The main idea is the most important *argument* being made by the author. The topic is shared in a few words while the main idea needs a full sentence to be understood. As an example, a short passage might have the topic of penguins, and the main idea could be written as *Penguins are different from other birds in many ways.*

In most nonfiction writing, the topic and the main idea will be stated clearly. Sometimes, they will come in a sentence at the very beginning or end of the passage. When you want to know the topic, you frequently find it in the first sentence of each paragraph. A body paragraph's first sentence is often--but not always--the topic sentence. The topic sentence gives you a summary of the ideas in the paragraph. You may find that the topic or main idea is not given clearly. So, you must read every sentence of the passage. Then, try to come up with an overall idea from each sentence.

Note: A thesis statement is not the same as the main idea. The main idea gives a brief, general summary of a text. The thesis statement gives a clear idea on an issue that is backed up with evidence.

> **Review Video: Topics and Main Ideas**
> Visit mometrix.com/academy and enter code: 407801

## PASSAGE STRUCTURE FOR NON-NARRATIVE PASSAGES

### TITLE

Centered on the page, the title's main words are capitalized (articles, prepositions, and infinitives are not capitalized in a title). The title may have quotation marks, or it may be underlined or italicized. The title has a few words that hint at the subject of the paper and catch the reader's interest.

### INTRODUCTION

An introduction summarizes the passage and the thesis statement. The purpose of the introduction is to grab the reader's attention. To do this, authors may use a quote, question, or strong opinion. Some authors choose to use an interesting description or puzzling statement. Also, authors use the introduction to explain their reason for writing.

### BODY PARAGRAPH

Following the introduction, body paragraphs are used to explain the thesis statement. A body paragraph has a topic sentence, typically the first sentence. In these paragraphs, there is evidence that helps the argument of the paragraph. Also, the author may give commentary on the evidence. Be careful because this commentary can be filled with bias.

The topic sentence gives the paragraph's subject and the main idea. The rest of the body paragraph should be linked to the topic sentence. Again, the topic sentence should be supported with facts, details, and examples.

The topic sentence is general and covers the ideas in a body paragraph. Sometimes, the topic sentence may be implied (i.e., the sentence is not stated directly by the author). Also, the topic sentence shows the connections among the supporting details.

22

## CONCLUSION

The conclusion should provide a summary on the passage. New material is not given in the conclusion. The conclusion is the final paragraph that may have a call to action (something the writer wants readers to do) or a question for the reader to think about.

The main idea is the umbrella argument of a passage. So, **supporting details** back up the main idea. To show that a main idea is correct, authors add details that prove their idea. All passages contain details. However, they are supporting details when they help an argument in the passage. Supporting details are found in informative and persuasive texts. Sometimes they will come with terms like *for example* or *for instance*. Or, they will be numbered with terms like *first*, *second*, and *last*. You should think about how the author's supporting details back up his or her main idea. Supporting details can be factual yet biased toward the author's main idea. Sometimes supporting details can seem helpful. However, they may be useless when they are based on opinions.

**Review Video: Supporting Details**
Visit mometrix.com/academy and enter code: 396297

An example of a main idea is: *Giraffes live in the Serengeti of Africa.* A supporting detail about giraffes could be: *A giraffe in the Serengeti benefits from a long neck by reaching twigs and leaves on tall trees.* The main idea gives the general idea that the text is about giraffes. The supporting detail gives a clear fact about how the giraffes eat.

A **theme** is an issue, an idea, or a question raised by a passage. For example, a theme of *Cinderella* is determination as Cinderella serves her stepsisters and stepmother. Passages may have many themes, so be careful to find only themes that you are asked to find. One common mark of themes is that they give more questions than answers. Authors try to push readers to consider themes in other ways. You can find themes by asking about the general problems that the passage is addressing. A good way to find a theme is to begin reading with a question in mind (e.g., How does this passage use the theme of love?) and to look for answers to that question.

**Review Video: Theme**
Visit mometrix.com/academy and enter code: 732074

## EVALUATING A PASSAGE

When you read informational passages, you need to make a conclusion from the author's writing. You can **identify a logical conclusion** (find a conclusion that makes sense) to know whether you agree or disagree with an author. Coming to this conclusion is like making an inference: you combine the information from the passage with what you already know. From the passage's information and your knowledge, you can come to a conclusion that makes sense. One way to have a conclusion that makes sense is to take notes of all the author's points. When the notes are organized, they may point to the logical conclusion. Another way to reach conclusions is to ask if the author's passage raises any helpful questions. Sometimes you will be able to draw many conclusions from a passage. Yet, these may be conclusions that were never imagined by the author. Therefore, find reasons in the passage for the conclusions that you make.

**Review Video: Identifying Logical Conclusions**
Visit mometrix.com/academy and enter code: 281653

**Text evidence** is the information that supports a main argument or minor argument. This evidence, or proof, can lead you to a conclusion. Information used as text evidence is clear, descriptive, and full of facts. Supporting details give evidence to back up an argument.

For example, a passage may state that winter occurs during opposite months in the Northern hemisphere (north of the equator) and Southern hemisphere (south of the equator). Text evidence for this claim may include a list of countries where winter occurs in opposite months. Also, you may be given reasons that winter occurs at different times of the year in these hemispheres (such as the tilt of the earth as it rotates around the sun).

> **Review Video: Text Evidence**
> Visit mometrix.com/academy and enter code: 486236

A text is **credible**, or believable, when the author is knowledgeable and fair. The author's motivations for writing the passage have an important part in judging the credibility of the passage. For example, passages written about a professional soccer game by a sports reporter and an average fan will have different levels of credibility.

A reader should always draw **conclusions** from passages. Sometimes conclusions are implied (i.e., information that is assumed) from written information. Other times the information is **stated directly** within the passage. You should try to draw conclusions from information stated in a passage. Furthermore, you should always read through the entire passage before drawing conclusions. Readers often expect the author's conclusions at the beginning or the end of the passage. However, many texts do not follow this format.

**Implications** are things that the author does not say directly, but you can assume from what the author does say. For example: *I stepped outside and opened my umbrella. By the time I got to work, the cuffs of my pants were soaked.* The author never says that it is raining. However, you can conclude that this information is implied. Conclusions from implications must be well supported by the passage. To draw a conclusion, you should have many pieces of proof. If you have only one piece of evidence, then you need to be sure that there is no other possible explanation than your conclusion. Practice drawing conclusions from implications in real life events to improve your skills.

**Outlining** the information in a passage should be a familiar skill to readers. A good outline will show the pattern of the passage and lead to better conclusions. A common outline lists the main ideas of the passage in the order that they come. Then, beneath each main idea, you can list the minor ideas and details. An outline does not need to include every detail from the passage. However, the outline should show everything that is important to the argument.

Another helpful tool is **summarizing** information. This process is similar to creating an outline. First, a summary should define the main idea of the passage. The summary should have the most important supporting details or arguments. Summaries can be unclear or wrong because they do not stay true to the information in the passage. A helpful summary should have the same message as the passage.

Ideas from a passage can be organized using **graphic organizers**. A graphic organizer reduces information to a few key points. A graphic organizer like a timeline may have an event listed for each date on the timeline. However, an outline may have an event listed under a key point that happens in the passage.

Make a graphic organizer that works best for you. Whatever helps you remember information from a passage is what you need to use. A spider-map is another example. This map takes a main idea from the story and places it in a bubble. From one main idea bubble, you put supporting points that connect to the main idea. A Venn diagram groups information as separate or connected with some overlap.

**Paraphrasing** is another method that you can use to understand a passage. To paraphrase, you put what you have read into your own words. Or, you can *translate* what the author shared into your words by including as many details as you can.

## RESPONDING TO A PASSAGE

One part of being a good reader is making predictions. A **prediction** is a guess about what will happen next. Readers make predictions from what they have read and what they already know. For example: *Staring at the computer screen in shock, Kim reached for the glass of water.* The sentence leaves you to think that she is not looking at the glass. So, you may guess that Kim is going to knock over the glass. Yet in the next sentence you may read that Kim does not knock over the glass. As you have more information, be ready for your predictions to change.

*Test-taking tip*: To respond to questions that ask about predictions, your answer should come from the passage.

You will be asked to understand text that gives ideas without stating them directly. An **inference** is something that is implied but not stated directly by the author. For example: *After the final out of the inning, the fans were filled with joy and rushed the field.* From this sentence, you can infer that the fans were watching baseball and their team won. You should not use information outside of the passage before making inferences. As you practice making inferences, you will find that they need all of your attention.

*Test-taking tip*: When asked about inferences, look for **context clues**. Context is what surrounds the words and sentences, adding explanation or information to an unknown piece. An answer can be *true* but not *correct*. The context clues will help you find the answer that is best. When asked for the implied meaning of a statement, you should locate the statement first. Then, read the context around the statement. Finally, look for an answer with a similar phrase.

For your exam, you must be able to find a text's **sequence** (i.e., the order that things happen). When the sequence is very important to the author, the passage comes with signal words: *first, then, next,* and *last*. However, a sequence can be implied. For example, *He walked through the garden and gave water and fertilizer to the plants.* Clearly, the man did not walk through the garden at the beginning. First, he found water. Then, he collected fertilizer. Next, he walked through the garden. Finally, he gave water and fertilizer to the plants. Passages do not always come in a clear sequence. Sometimes they begin at the end. Or, they can begin halfway through and then start over at the beginning. You can strengthen your understanding of the passage by taking notes to understand the sequence.

**Dual passages**, or comparative essays, give two passages from authors with different points of view. The format of the two passages will change with each exam. For example, the author of the first passage may give an idea from his or her point of view. Then, the author of the second passage gives an argument against the first passage. Other dual passages will give a topic in the first passage. Then the second passage will support or provide explanation for the topic in the first passage.

You may see that the questions ask about passage one, passage two, and both passages. No matter the length or kind of passages, you should read them in order (read Passage 1 first, then move on to Passage 2). However, if your time is limited, you can read passage 1 first and answer all of the questions for passage 1. Then, read passage 2 and answer the remaining questions.

# Building a Vocabulary

Learning the basics of language is helpful in understanding what you read. **Structural analysis** means to break a word into pieces to find its definition. Parts of a word include prefixes, suffixes, and root words. Knowing the meanings of these parts can help you understand the definition of a difficult word.

The main part of a word is known as the root. Prefixes are common letter combinations at the beginning of words. Suffixes are common letter combinations at the ends of words. In pieces, a word looks like this: prefix + root word + suffix. First, look at the individual definitions of the root word, prefix, and/or suffix. Then, see how they add to the root. You can use knowledge of a prefix's and/or suffix's definition to determine a close definition of the word. For example, if you don't know the definition of *uninspired* you may be able to figure it out because you know that *un-* means 'not.' Thus, the full word means *not inspired*. Learning the common prefixes and suffixes can help you define difficult words.

> **Review Video: <u>Determining Word Meanings</u>**
> Visit mometrix.com/academy and enter code: 894894

Below is a list of common prefixes and their meanings:

## PREFIXES FOR NUMBERS

| Prefix | Definition | Examples |
| --- | --- | --- |
| Bi- | Two | bisect, biennial, bicycle |
| Mono- | One, single | monogamy, monologue, monopoly |
| Poly- | Many | polymorphous, polygamous, polygon |
| Semi- | Half, partly | semicircle, semicolon, semiannually |
| Uni- | one | uniform, unity, unanimous |
| a- | in, on, of, up, to | abed, afoot |
| ab- | from, away, off | abdicate, abjure |
| ad- | to, toward | advance, adventure |
| ante- | before, previous | antecedent, antedate |
| anti- | against, opposing | antipathy, antidote |
| cata- | down, away, thorou | catastrophe, cataclysm |
| circum- | around | circumspect, circumferen |
| com- | with, together, very | commotion, complicate |
| contra- | against, opposing | contradict, contravene |
| de- | from | depart |
| dia- | through, across, apa | diameter, diagnose |
| dis- | away, off, down, not | dissent, disappear |
| epi- | upon | epilogue |
| ex- | out | extract, excerpt |
| hypo- | under, beneath | hypodermic, hypothesis |
| inter- | among, between | intercede, interrupt |
| intra- | within | intramural, intrastate |
| ob- | against, opposing | objection |
| per- | through | perceive, permit |
| peri- | around | periscope, perimeter |
| post- | after, following | postpone, postscript |
| pre- | before, previous | prevent, preclude |
| pro- | forward, in place of | propel, pronoun |
| retro- | back, backward | retrospect, retrograde |
| sub- | under, beneath | subjugate, substitute |
| super- | above, extra | supersede, supernumerar |
| trans- | across, beyond, ove | transact, transport |
| ultra- | beyond, excessively | ultramodern, ultrasonic |

28

## PREFIXES FOR TIME, DIRECTION, AND SPACE

| Prefix | Definition | Examples |
|--------|------------|----------|
| a- | in, on, of, up, to | abed, afoot |
| ab- | from, away, off | abdicate, abjure |
| ad- | to, toward | advance, adventure |
| ante- | before, previous | antecedent, antedate |
| anti- | against, opposing | antipathy, antidote |
| cata- | down, away, thorou | catastrophe, cataclysm |
| circum | around | circumspect, circumferen |
| com- | with, together, very | commotion, complicate |
| contra- | against, opposing | contradict, contravene |
| de- | from | depart |
| dia- | through, across, apa | diameter, diagnose |
| dis- | away, off, down, not | dissent, disappear |
| epi- | upon | epilogue |
| ex- | out | extract, excerpt |
| hypo- | under, beneath | hypodermic, hypothesis |
| inter- | among, between | intercede, interrupt |
| intra- | within | intramural, intrastate |
| ob- | against, opposing | objection |
| per- | through | perceive, permit |
| peri- | around | periscope, perimeter |
| post- | after, following | postpone, postscript |
| pre- | before, previous | prevent, preclude |
| pro- | forward, in place of | propel, pronoun |
| retro- | back, backward | retrospect, retrograde |
| sub- | under, beneath | subjugate, substitute |
| super- | above, extra | supersede, supernumera |
| trans- | across, beyond, over | transact, transport |
| ultra- | beyond, excessively | ultramodern, ultrasonic |

## NEGATIVE PREFIXES

| Prefix | Definition | Examples |
|---|---|---|
| a- | without, lacking | atheist, agnostic |
| in- | not, opposing | incapable, ineligible |
| non- | not | nonentity, nonsense |
| un- | not, reverse of | unhappy, unlock |

## EXTRA PREFIXES

| Prefix | Definition | Examples |
|---|---|---|
| belli- | war, warlike | bellicose |
| bene- | well, good | benefit, benefactor |
| equi- | equal | equivalent, equilibrium |
| for- | away, off, from | forget, forswear |
| fore- | previous | foretell, forefathers |
| homo- | same, equal | homogenized, homonym |
| hyper- | excessive, over | hypercritical, hypertension |
| in- | in, into | intrude, invade |
| magn- | large | magnitude, magnify |
| mal- | bad, poorly, not | malfunction, malpractice |
| mis- | bad, poorly, not | misspell, misfire |
| mor- | death | mortality, mortuary |
| neo- | new | Neolithic, neoconservative |
| omni- | all, everywhere | omniscient, omnivore |
| ortho- | right, straight | orthogonal, orthodox |
| over- | above | overbearing, oversight |
| pan- | all, entire | panorama, pandemonium |
| para- | beside, beyond | parallel, paradox |
| phil- | love, like | philosophy, philanthropic |
| prim- | first, early | primitive, primary |
| re- | backward, again | revoke, recur |
| sym- | with, together | sympathy, symphony |
| vis- | to see | visage, visible |

Below is a list of common suffixes and their meanings:

## ADJECTIVE SUFFIXES

| Suffix | Definition | Examples |
|---|---|---|
| -able (-ible) | capable of being | toler*able*, ed*ible* |
| -esque | in the style of, like | picturesque, grotesque |
| -ful | filled with, marked by | thankful, zestful |
| -ic | make, cause | terrific, beatific |
| -ish | suggesting, like | churlish, childish |
| -less | lacking, without | hopeless, countless |
| -ous | marked by, given to | religious, riotous |

## NOUN SUFFIXES

| Suffix | Definition | Examples |
|---|---|---|
| -acy | state, condition | accuracy, privacy |
| -ance | act, condition, fact | acceptance, vigilance |
| -ard | one that does excessively | drunkard, sluggard |
| -ation | action, state, result | occupation, starvation |
| -dom | state, rank, condition | serfdom, wisdom |
| -er (-or) | office, action | teach*er*, elevat*or*, hon*or* |
| -ess | feminine | waitress, duchess |
| -hood | state, condition | manhood, statehood |
| -ion | action, result, state | union, fusion |
| -ism | act, manner, doctrine | barbarism, socialism |
| -ist | worker, follower | monopolist, socialist |
| -ity (-ty) | state, quality, condition | acid*ity*, civil*ity*, twen*ty* |
| -ment | result, action | refreshment |
| -ness | quality, state | greatness, tallness |
| -ship | position | internship, statesmanship |
| -sion (-tion) | state, result | revi*sion*, expedi*tion* |
| -th | act, state, quality | warmth, width |
| -tude | quality, state, result | magnitude, fortitude |

## VERB SUFFIXES

| Suffix | Definition | Examples |
|--------|-----------|----------|
| -ate | having, showing | separate, desolate |
| -en | cause to be, become | deepen, strengthen |
| -fy | make, cause to have | glorify, fortify |
| -ize | cause to be, treat with | sterilize, mechanize |

**Review Video: English Root Words**
Visit mometrix.com/academy and enter code: 896380

There is more to a word than the dictionary definition. The **denotative** meaning of a word is the actual meaning found in a dictionary. For example, a house and a home are places where people live. The **connotative meaning** is what comes to mind when you think of a word. For example, a house may be a simple, solid building. Yet, a home may be a comfortable, welcoming place where a family dwells. Most nonfiction is fact-based with no use of figurative language. So, you can assume that the writer will use denotative meanings. In fiction, drama, and poetry, the author may use the connotative meaning. Use context clues to know if the author is using the denotative or connotative meaning of a word.

**Review Video: Denotation and Connotation**
Visit mometrix.com/academy and enter code: 310092

Readers of all levels will find new words in passages. The best way to define a word in **context** is to think about the words that are around the unknown word. For example, nouns that you don't know may be followed by examples that give a definition. Think about this example: *Dave arrived at the party in hilarious garb: a leopard-print shirt, buckskin pants, and tennis shoes.* If you didn't know the meaning of 'garb,' you could read the examples (leopard-print shirt, buckskin pants, and tennis shoes) and know that *garb* means *clothing*. Examples will not always be this clear. Try another example: *Parsley, lemon, and flowers were just a few of items he used as garnishes.* The word *garnishes* is explained by parsley, lemon, and flowers. From this one sentence, you may infer that the items are used for decoration. Are they decorating a food plate or an ice table with meat? You would need the other sentences in the paragraph to know for sure.

**Review Video: Context**
Visit mometrix.com/academy and enter code: 613660

Also, you can use contrasts to define an unfamiliar word in context. In many sentences, authors will not describe the unfamiliar word directly. Instead, they will describe the opposite of the unfamiliar word. So, you are given some information that will bring you closer to defining the word. For example: *Despite his intelligence, Hector's bad posture made him look obtuse. Despite* means that Hector's posture is at odds with his intelligence. The author explains that Hector's posture does not prove his intelligence. So, *obtuse* must mean *unintelligent.* Another example: *Even with the horrible weather, we were beatific about our trip to Alaska.* The weather is described as *horrible.* So, *beatific* must mean something positive.

Sometimes, there will be very few context clues to help you define an unknown word. When this happens, **substitution** is a helpful tool. First, try to think of some synonyms for the words. Then, use those synonyms in place of the unknown words. If the passage makes sense, then the substitution has given some information about the unknown word. For example: *Frank's admonition rang in her ears as she climbed the mountain.* If you don't know the definition of *admonition*, try some substitutions: *vow, promise, advice, complaint,* or *compliment*. These words hint that an *admonition* is some sort of message. Once in a while substitution can get you a precise definition.

Usually you can define an unfamiliar word by looking at the descriptive words in the context. For example: *Fred dragged the recalcitrant boy, kicking and screaming, up the stairs.* The words *dragged, kicking,* and *screaming* all hint that the boy hates going up the stairs. So, you may deduce that *recalcitrant* means something like unwilling or protesting. In this example, an unfamiliar adjective was identified. Contrasts do not always give detailed information about the unknown word. However, they do give you some clues to understand it.

**Description** is used more to define an unfamiliar noun than unfamiliar adjectives. For example: *Don's wrinkled frown and constantly shaking fist labeled him as a curmudgeon.* Don is described as having a *wrinkled frown* and *constantly shaking fist.* This hints that a *curmudgeon* must be a grumpy, old man.

Many words have more than one **definition**. So you may not know how the word is being used in a sentence. For example, the verb *cleave* can mean *join* or *separate*. When you see this word, you need to pick the definition that makes the most sense. For example: *The birds cleaved together as they flew from the oak tree.* The use of the word *together* hints that *cleave* is being used to mean *join*. Another example: *Hermione's knife cleaved the bread cleanly.* A knife cannot join bread together. So, the word must hint at separation. Learning the purpose of a word with many meanings needs the same tricks as defining an unknown word. Look for context clues and try substituting words.

To learn more from a passage, you need to understand how words connect to each other. This is done with understanding **synonyms** (e.g., words that mean the same thing) and **antonyms** (e.g., the opposite meaning of a word). For example, *dry* and *arid* are synonyms. However, *dry* and *wet* are antonyms. There are pairs of words in English that can be called synonyms, yet they have somewhat different definitions. For example, *friendly* and *collegial* can be used to describe a warm, close relationship. So, you would be correct to call them synonyms. However, *collegial* (linked to *colleague*) is used for professional or academic relationships. *Friendly* is not linked to professional or academic relationships.

Words should not be called synonyms when their differences are too great. For example, *hot* and *warm* are not synonyms because their meanings are too different. How do you know when two words are synonyms? First, try to replace one word for the other word. Then, be sure that the meaning of the sentence has not changed. Replacing *warm* for *hot* in a sentence gives a different meaning. *Warm* and *hot* may seem close in meaning. Yet *warm* means that the temperature is normal, while *hot* means that the temperature is very high.

Antonyms are words with opposite meanings. *Light* and *dark, up* and *down, right* and *left, good* and *bad* are sets of antonyms. However, there is a difference between antonyms and pairs of words that are different. *Black* and *gray* are not antonyms, because *black* is not the opposite of *gray*. On the other hand, *black* and *white* are antonyms. Not every word has an antonym. For example, many nouns do not have an antonym. What would be the antonym of *chair*?

33

During your exam, the questions about antonyms are likely to be about adjectives. Remember that adjectives are words that describe a noun. Some common adjectives include *red*, *fast*, *skinny*, and *sweet*. From these four adjectives, *red* is the one that does not have an antonym.

**Review Video: <u>Synonyms and Antonyms</u>**
Visit mometrix.com/academy and enter code: 105612

# Listening

The Listening section of the TOEFL consists of a total of 28-39 questions and will last between 41 and 57 minutes. There will be 3-4 lectures with 6 questions each and 2-3 conversations with 5 questions each.

There are three types of questions:

1. short conversations
2. long conversations and class discussions
3. lectures

You will have a headset that will allow you to adjust the volume of the recording. Short conversations will begin with a picture to provide orientation. With longer conversations and lectures, you will be provided with several pictures and visual cues.

## Tips for the Listening Section

The listening section requires you to demonstrate your ability to understand verbal information and use pragmatic understanding to interpret content, tone, and purpose.

### TIP 1: LISTENING FOR BASIC COMPREHENSION

When preparing for the test, take some time to find English radio, lectures, podcasts, and videos to watch and listen to. You should pick different types of sources because during this section of the test, you will be exposed to both academic and everyday English. Practice taking mental notes of what is said and try listening for main points.

### TIP 2: LISTENING FOR PRAGMATIC UNDERSTANDING

Speakers use tone and emphasis in speech to create a certain mood or to accomplish a certain goal. After you are comfortable with listening for basic comprehension, try listening for tone and try to identify a speaker's purpose. Try also to identify whether a speaker is talking more casually or informatively and if there is a particular emotion conveyed.

### TIP 3: CONNECTING AND SYNTHESIZING INFORMATION

As you listen to speakers talk, you will have to connect information to form conclusions. Try to notice if two speakers make opposing points or if there is a reason behind what is said. After you listen to a sample of speech, practice summarizing and restating information, then listen again to check yourself.

## Listening Skills

### USE THE PICTURES

The pictures are provided to orient you to the atmosphere and environment in which the speakers are conducting their conversation. Use those pictures as much as possible. Try to put yourself in that environment. Become one of the pictured speakers and you will be able to better appreciate the conversation and what it means.

## USE MULTIPLE INPUTS

The questions will be read to you at the same time they are exposed on the screen in the form of text. Take advantage of this. Use both the visual and auditory information being presented to better understand what is being asked. Some people are better visual and some better auditory receivers of information. Since both methods of presenting questions are given, use them both to your maximum advantage.

## MAIN IDEAS

Important words and main ideas in conversation are ones that will come up again and again. Listen carefully for any word or words that come up repeatedly. What words come up in nearly every statement made? These words with high frequency are likely to be in the main idea of the conversation. For example, in a conversation about class size in the business department of a college, the term "class size" is likely to appear in nearly every statement made by either speaker in the discussion.

## VOICE CHANGES

On the TOEFL, you are expected to be able to recognize and interpret nuances of speech. Be on the alert for any changes in voice, which might register surprise, excitement, or another emotion. If a speaker is talking in a normal monotone voice and suddenly raises their voice to a high pitch, that is a huge clue that something critical is being stated. Listen for a speaker to change their voice and understand the meaning of what they are saying.

Example:

Man: Let's go to Wal-mart.

Woman: *There's a Wal-mart in this small town?*

If the woman's statement was higher pitched, indicating surprise and shock, then she probably did not expect there to be a Wal-mart in that town.

Speakers may also place stronger stress on words that are important, which helps in understanding the focal point of a sentence or can even change sentence meaning.

Example:

Man: Did *you* play baseball over the weekend?

Woman: *We* didn't play baseball. We *watched* a baseball game over the weekend.

Example:

Man: Did you play *baseball* over the weekend?

Woman: We didn't play *baseball;* we played *tennis* instead.

In these examples, the subject of the man's question changes based on which word receives the stress.

## SPECIFICS

Listen carefully for specific pieces of information. Adjectives are commonly asked about in TOEFL questions. Try to remember any main adjectives that are mentioned. Pick out adjectives such as numbers, colors, or sizes.

Example:

Man: Let's go to the store and get some apples to make the pie.

Woman: How many do we need?

Man: We'll need **five** apples to make the pie.

A typical question might be about how many apples were needed.

## INTERPRET

As you are listening to the conversation, put yourself in the person's shoes. Think about why someone would make a statement. You'll need to do more than just regurgitate the spoken words; you must also interpret them.

Example:

Woman: I think I'm sick with the flu.

Man: Why don't you go see the campus doctor?

Sample Question: Why did the man mention the campus doctor?

Answer: The campus doctor would be able to determine if the woman had the flu.

## FIND THE HIDDEN MEANING

Look for the meaning behind a statement. When a speaker answers a question with a statement that doesn't immediately seem to answer the question, the response probably contains a hidden meaning that you will need to recognize and explain.

Man: Are you going to be ready for your presentation?

Woman: I've only got half of it finished and it's taken me five hours just to do this much. There's only an hour left before the presentation is due.

At first, the woman did not seem to answer the question the man presented. She responded with a statement that only seemed loosely related. Once you look deeper, then you can find the true meaning of what she said. If it took the woman five hours to do the first half of the presentation, then it would logically take her another five hours to do the second half. Since she only has one hour

until her presentation is due, she would probably NOT be ready for the presentation. So, while an answer was not immediately visible to the man's question, when you applied logic to her response, you could find the hidden meaning.

# Types of Listening Problems

## TYPES OF CONVERSATIONS ON THE TOEFL

On your test, you will encounter a variety of listening prompts which may include one or more speakers. These may include more academic or more informal speakers who may either agree or disagree with one another. You must be able to determine main ideas and viewpoints when encountering conversations.

## ACADEMIC CONVERSATIONS

Academic conversations are conversations on a college campus between professors, students, and other campus members. You will need to be able to summarize main ideas and recall important details.

## CLASS DISCUSSIONS

Class discussions are conversations in a classroom between professors and students. You will need to be able to summarize main ideas, but usually NOT need to recall important details.

## ACADEMIC TALKS

Academic talks are conversations in an orientation meeting on academic courses and procedures or where a professor might discuss a variety of college topics. You will need to be able to summarize main ideas, but usually NOT need to recall important details.

## LECTURES

Lectures are conversations in a classroom about academic topics. You will need to be able to summarize main ideas, and be able to answer questions such as: who, what, when, where, or why?

## ACTIVE LISTENING

Although listening appears to be a passive process, it must be **active** in order to be effective. Indeed, the listener should have a **purpose** for listening. The precise purpose of listening need not be conscious in the mind of the listener. In general, there are four distinguished **intentions** of listening: comprehension, criticism, empathy, and appreciation. These intentions are often intermingled in the same act of listening. When we listen for comprehension, we are trying to understand the message the speaker is communicating. In order to listen for comprehension, we need to know the standards of grammar and punctuation in English. We also need to know the common forms of argument. We also need to have an understanding of the context in which the words are spoken so that we can understand the relationship between message and context.

## LISTENING FOR THE PURPOSES OF CRITICISM

In order to listen for the purposes of criticism, one must usually also be listening for **comprehension**. It is true that in order to accurately assess the quality of a verbal communication, you will need to understand the content of the communication first. To a certain degree, however, we all apply critical listening skills to communication we have yet to fully understand. For instance, when we hear an advertisement on the radio, we know immediately that the speaker is trying to sell us something, and so we are naturally receptive or skeptical of the message, depending on our

38

preexisting interest in the product or service. In this case, our **critical listening skills** are influencing our listening even before we have begun to comprehend the content.

## LISTENING FOR CONTENT

In almost every listening situation, the audience is required to listen for **information**. A communication can only be considered effective if the message communicates the information intended by the speaker. The **feedback** issued by the audience indicates the degree to which the information has been received accurately. When the audience is required to ask for clarification or repetition of the message, it is possible that the speaker has been ineffective in delivering his or her information. Moreover, if the audience provides no verbal feedback about a delivered message, it is possible that they either do not understand any of the message or are simply not interested in it. Of course, when there is no verbal feedback it is also possible that the audience simply understands the transmitted message perfectly and requires no clarification or elaboration.

## LISTENING FOR COMPREHENSION

There are five basic kinds of **intentional listening**: appreciative, therapeutic, discriminative, comprehensive, and critical. **Listening for comprehension** is probably the most familiar form of listening. Students in a classroom are engaged in listening for comprehension when they take notes during a lecture. Whenever we listen to an informative or persuasive speech in order to obtain information about a subject, we are engaged in listening for comprehension. The validity and accuracy of other forms of listening, such as critical listening and discriminative listening, depend on effective listening for comprehension. If an individual is unable to understand the message that is being presented, he or she will not be able to critique it insightfully.

## ASSESSING THE CHARACTERISTICS OF THE SPEAKER

As part of the overall critique of a speech, an audience member should consider the personal **characteristics of the speaker**. For instance, the audience member might consider what he or she knew about the speaker before the speech, and then decide whether this information had any influence on his or her interpretation of the speaker's message. The audience member might also consider whether the speaker's personal presentation indicated credibility or made his or her message difficult to believe. Many times, a speaker with a good message and solid supporting materials comes across as vague and disorganized because of his or her physical appearance and vocal mannerisms. Audience members should try to distinguish between weaknesses in the speaker's message and weaknesses in the speaker's personal presentation.

## ANALYZING THE MESSAGE OF THE SPEECH

When an audience member listens to a speech, he or she should be attending to three fundamental **factors**: ideas, organization, and support. The most important thing to consider is whether the speaker's main ideas are *logical and clearly expressed*. If the ideas are comprehensible, an audience member can then consider whether they have been expressed in the *logical order*, or whether the speaker has presented them in a disorganized fashion. Finally, the audience member needs to consider whether the speaker's main ideas have been adequately *supported* by argument or factual evidence. Does the speaker provide enough support for his arguments to remain credible? Is the evidence provided relevant to the main ideas of the speech?

# Speaking

In the speaking section, a topic will be presented to you and you must provide a short speech in response to the topic. Both the preparation and the speech must take place within the time allowed. There is not a correct answer to the topic. You must evaluate the topic, organize your ideas, and develop them into a cohesive and coherent response.

In one of the four tasks you will have to perform will be **independent speaking** and three will involve an **integrated reading and listening** section.

You will be scored on how well you are able to utilize standard spoken English, organize and explain your thoughts, and speak clearly to address the question.

Of all the test sections on the TOEFL, this is the easiest to prepare for. This is the test section that you can practice anywhere, in your car, in your room, on the phone, by yourself, or with someone else. After you successfully pass TOEFL, you will be speaking English a lot, so you might as well prepare by speaking it at every opportunity beforehand.

## Tips for the Speaking Section

The speaking section will require you to demonstrate your ability to speak English in both academic and informal settings. This involves speaking in an organized and clear manner without much preparation time. You will be asked to give four short speeches ranging from 45 to 60 seconds regarding a variety of topics.

### TIP 1: ANSWERING THE QUESTION

The speaking section of the test provides you with very little time to accomplish your goal of answering a question. Make sure that you spend your time saying things that matter and avoid saying things that do not. To practice, record yourself speaking about familiar topics. Go back and listen to yourself and identify unnecessary information. Try answering again until you think you have answered the question without digressing.

### TIP 2: SPEAKING CLEARLY

A major part of speech requires you to pace yourself and speak not too quickly or too slowly. Speakers should also place adequate emphasis on key words, such as important nouns and verbs in each sentence. For practice, record yourself speaking or have someone listen to you and point out areas that are confusing.

### TIP 3: GRAMMATICAL ACCURACY

While speaking, grammatical accuracy plays a key point in clearly communicating what you mean. Try recording your responses to questions about familiar topics, and write down your answers or listen for grammatical errors. To help keep your grammar clear, make your points simple rather than complex.

### TIP 4: ORGANIZATION

Similar to the way writing should be organized with an introduction, three main points, and a conclusion, short speeches should be organized to make sure that everything that is said is to the point or supports the main objective. Practice making short arguments with clear points.

## TIP 5: USING TIME EFFECTIVELY

Remember that the speaking section provides you with only 15 seconds to prepare and 45 seconds to answer the questions. Practice timing yourself answering questions and take note if you are speaking too quickly or including unnecessary information. Try practicing with a variety of topics.

## PRACTICE TIPS:

- Make and practice a list of familiar topics and a few that you may not know much about.
- Verbally practice retelling specific days (yesterday, a holiday, etc.). Make sure to practice using prepositions and other connecting words, such as first, next, then, throughout.
- Practice telling short stories from your experiences in under a minute.
- Read or listen to a story and retell it.

Record yourself and ask yourself the following questions:

- Did I complete the task?
- Did I speak clearly?
- Did I make any grammatical errors?
- Were my points organized?
- Did I use my time well?

# Preparing to Speak

## BRAINSTORM

Spend your preparation time thinking of your main answer and a few points supporting your conclusion, as if this were a written response. Time is key, so do not try to think of too many reasons, but only what can be explained simply and clearly.

## THE CLEAR MESSAGE OF A SPEECH

When speaking, you should be focusing on three fundamental **factors**: ideas, organization, and support. The most important thing for you to consider is whether the main ideas are *logical and clearly expressed*. If the ideas are comprehensible, you should then consider whether they have been expressed in the *logical order*, or whether you have presented them in a disorganized fashion. Finally, you need to consider whether your main ideas have been adequately *supported* by logic or facts. Do you provide enough support for your arguments to remain credible? Is the evidence provided relevant to the main ideas?

## EXHAUSTING THE POSSIBILITIES

You will be prompted with some basic questions. There are only so many possible basic questions that can be asked about someone, so you can easily be prepared for every possibility. Go through and write down all the possibilities and a good answer for each. When you're asked about your family, you don't have to struggle to come up with descriptions for your family members. Practice ahead of time and know what you're going to say. Right now, as you're reading this, stop and take a minute to answer each of the following questions. If these were asked in an interview, what would you say?

1. Please describe yourself.
2. Please describe your family.
3. Please describe your home.
4. Please describe some of your interests.

5. Please describe your job.
6. Please describe your studies.

This is important practice. Make sure that you can spend a minute or so answering each of these questions without having to take time to think of a good response. These are basic questions and you should have your basic answers ready.

## TELL A STORY

Think about your favorite relatives. In many cases, they are your favorite because they are such raconteurs, or good storytellers. These are your aunts and uncles that can turn a simple trip to the grocery store into high adventure and keep you captivated and entertained. Even if you're not a natural storyteller, with a little thought and practice, even you can turn dull past experiences into exciting exploits.

**Stories** are your strongest weapon for demonstrating your mastery of speaking English. Some questions practically beg for stories to be told. These need to be compelling stories, real time drama, with you as the hero. Once you begin a quick, exciting story, you have set the tone.

The easiest way to prepare for these more difficult questions is to scour your memory for any exciting instance in your **past**, perhaps where you played a leadership role or accomplished a goal. This can be from any part of your past: during your education, at home with your family, doing a project at work, or anything that you might have had a part in. Identify the main characteristics of the story so you have the details correct. Make sure you know the basics of what happened, who was involved, why it occurred, and how the events unfolded sequentially. You certainly don't want to stumble over the facts and repeat yourself during your response.

## ONE SIZE FITS ALL

These basic stories are building blocks. Just as a piece of lumber can be cut into many different shapes and have many completely unique uses, each of your stories does not only answer one unique question. Your stories are **one size fits all**. With practice you will find that you can use the same story to answer two seemingly unrelated questions.

For example, a question about teamwork and a question about working under pressure can both be answered by a story about your experience playing intramural basketball. The story could describe how you had to work as a team in order to get into the playoffs, spending time practicing together, coordinating plays, and whatever was necessary for the team to advance. Alternatively, the story could focus on the shots that you made that season in order to win the game in the last few seconds of play under enormous pressure. The basic story is the same: your experiences playing basketball.

The questions were different, but you **customized** the story to fit the question. With practice you should be able to answer almost any question with just a few stock stories that can be customized.

## FIND THE BRIDGES

Some questions will lend themselves more readily to a story than others. You must have a set of basic stories ready that can be modified to fit the occasion. You must "find the bridges" in the questions offered to make sure your stories get told.

In WWII, the US Army used Bailey bridges. Bailey bridges were made of prefabricated steel sections that were carried around and could be thrown together at a moment's notice, allowing the army to move quickly across any obstacle and get to their destination.

You need to find bridges, i.e. **opportunities to tell your stories**. Look for any chance to turn a standard question about anything, into a bridge to begin telling your story. For example, "What is your job title?"

On the surface that might not seem like the ideal bridge, but with a little insight your response might become:

"My job title is Product Line Manager. I am responsible for everything from the development of new products to the obsolescence of old products. Marketing, sales, engineering, and production of the entire product line fall under my responsibility. One of the products was even my own idea based on feedback I received from my interactions with our customers. In the first year, it alone had achieved a sales level of over…"

The key to remember is that just because a question is **closed-ended** (yes/no or one word answers), you don't have to answer it as a closed-ended question. Answer the question asked, but then find a way to develop your answer into a bridge to a good story of yours. With an open mind, the most closed-ended of questions can become a launch pad into a story.

## PRACTICE MAKES PERFECT

Don't try to answer every question spontaneously. You'll spend most of your time trying to think of what happened and repeating yourself. Beforehand, think of the classic stories you could tell and then **practice** going over them with your friends, explaining how you successfully achieved the goal or took charge and gave leadership to your group project. You don't want to have the story memorized, because it will become stale in the telling, but you want it to be smooth. This story must be live and in living color, so that a potential listener could see himself taking part and watching the situation unfold. Have your friends and family members quiz you by asking you random questions and see how well you can adapt to the question and give a clear response.

# Writing

You will have 50 minutes to complete two writing tasks during the writing section. The **integrated writing task** will involve reading and listening followed by a response. The **independent writing task** involves writing an argument supporting an opinion.

In each task, a topic will be presented to you and you must write out a discussion on it within the time allowed. You must evaluate the topic, organize your ideas, and develop them into a cohesive and coherent response.

These tasks will not necessarily have a right or a wrong answer. You will be scored on how well you are able to utilize standard written English, organize and explain your thoughts, and support those thoughts with reasons and examples.

## Tips for the Writing Section

For the writing section of this test, you will need to answer an integrated writing task, which involves a reading or speaking comprehension section with a writing response to the topic. The Independent writing task asks you to explain and support your own opinion about an issue.

### Tip 1: Integrated Writing Task

For the integrated writing task, you will need to understand and respond to written and **verbal input**. Try to take note of what is said so you can refer back to this information in your own responses for comparison or contrast.

### Tip 2: Independent Writing Task

For the independent writing task, you will need to write an essay explaining and supporting your own **opinion** regarding a subject. For this, you should try to be as organized as possible, making clear points and organizing them into meaningful paragraphs. Follow the introduction, body, and conclusion format if possible. Practice discussing common issues in this format and review your work to eliminate unnecessary information. Remember that extra information only slows down and can confuse readers.

### Tip 3: General Recommendations

Try to learn **descriptive adverbs and adjectives** that can be used in many arguments rather than using common words. Descriptive language can keep readers engaged and provide more detail if used correctly. Practice using a **QWERTY keyboard**, which you will need to use during this test.

## The Writing Process

### Brainstorm

Spend the first few minutes brainstorming ideas. Write down any ideas you might have on the topic. The purpose is to extract from the recesses of your memory any **relevant information**. In this stage, anything goes down. Write down any idea, regardless of how good or bad it may initially seem. You can use either the scratch paper provided or the word processor to quickly jot down your thoughts and ideas. The word processor is highly recommended though, particularly if you are a fast typist.

## STRENGTH THROUGH DIVERSITY

The best papers will contain **diversity** of examples and reasoning. As you brainstorm, consider different perspectives. Not only are there two sides to every topic, but there are also countless **perspectives** that can be considered. On any topic, different groups are impacted, with many reaching the same conclusion or position, but through vastly different paths. Try to "see" the topic through as many different eyes as you can. Look at it from every angle and vantage point. The more diverse the reasoning used, the more balanced the paper will become and the better the score will be.

*Example*:

The topic of free trade is not just two-sided. It impacts politicians, domestic (US) manufacturers, foreign manufacturers, the US economy, the world economy, strategic alliances, retailers, wholesalers, consumers, unions, workers, and the exchange not only of goods, but also of ideas, beliefs, and cultures. The more of these angles that you can use to approach the topic, the more solid your reasoning and the stronger your position.

Furthermore, don't just use information as to how the topic impacts other people. Draw liberally from your own **experience and observations**. Describe a personal experience that you have had and your own emotions from that moment. Anything you've seen in your community or observed in society can be expanded upon to further round out your position on the topic.

Once you have finished with your creative flow, stop and **review** it. Which idea allowed you to come up with the most supporting information? It's extremely important that you pick an angle that will allow you to have a thorough and comprehensive coverage of the topic. This is not about your personal convictions, but about writing a concise, rational discussion of an idea.

Every garden of ideas gets weeds in it. The ideas that you brainstormed are going to be random pieces of information of mixed value. Go through them methodically and pick out the ones that are the best. The best ideas are **strong points** that you can easily write a few sentences or a paragraph about.

Now that you know which ideas you are going to use and focus on, **organize** them. Put your writing points in a logical order. You have your main ideas that you will focus on, and must align them in a sequence that will flow in a smooth, sensible path from point to point, so that the reader will go smoothly from one idea to the next in a logical path. Readers must have a sense of continuity as they read your paper. You don't want a paper that rambles back and forth.

## START YOUR ENGINES

You have a logical flow of main ideas with which to start writing. Begin **expanding** on the topics in the sequence that you have set for yourself. Pace yourself. Don't spend too much time on any one of the ideas that you are expanding on. You want to have time for all of them. Make sure you watch your time. If you have twenty minutes left to write out your ideas and you have ten ideas, then you can only use two minutes per idea. It can be a daunting task to cram a lot of information down in words in a short amount of time, but if you pace yourself, you can get through it all. If you find that you are falling behind, speed up. Move through each idea more quickly, spending less time to expand upon the idea in order to catch up.

Once you finish expanding on each idea, go back to your brainstorming session up above, where you wrote out your ideas. Go ahead and scratch through the ideas as you write about them. This will let you see what you need to write about next, and also allow you to pace yourself and see what you have left to cover.

Your first paragraph should have several easily identifiable features.

- First, it should have a quick **description** or paraphrasing of the topic. Use your own words to briefly explain what the topic is about.
- Second, you should explain your **opinion** of the topic and give an explanation of why you feel that way. What is your decision or conclusion on the topic?
- Third, you should list your "writing points." What are the **main ideas** that you came up with earlier? This is your opportunity to outline the rest of your paper. Write a sentence explaining each idea that will be explained in further depth in additional paragraphs. If someone were only to read this paragraph, he or she should be able to get a good summary of the entire paper.

Each of your successive paragraphs should expand on one of the points listed in the main paragraph. Use your personal experience and knowledge to support each of your points. Everything should be backed up by **examples**.

Once you have finished expanding upon each of your main points, wrap it up. **Summarize** what you have said in a conclusion paragraph. Explain your opinion of the topic once more and quickly review why you feel that way. At this stage, you have already backed up your statements, so there is no need to do that again. All you are doing is refreshing the reader's mind on your main points.

## PUNCTUATION

If a section of text has an opening dash, parentheses, or comma at the beginning of a phrase, then you can be sure there should be a matching closing dash, parentheses, or comma at the end of the phrase. If items in a series are each separated by commas, then any additional items in that series will also need commas. Do not alternate punctuation. If a dash is at the beginning of a statement, then do not put a parenthesis at the ending of the statement.

## WORD CONFUSION

"Which" should be used to refer to things only.

*John's dog, which was called Max, is large and fierce.*

"That" may be used to refer to either persons or things.

*Is this the only book that Louis L'Amour wrote?*

*Is Louis L'Amour the author that [or who] wrote Western novels?*

"Who" should be used to refer to persons only.

*Mozart was the composer who [or that] wrote those operas.*

## PRONOUN USAGE

To determine the correct pronoun form in a compound subject, try each subject separately with the verb, adapting the form as necessary. Your ear will tell you which form is correct.

Example: *Bob and (I, me) will be going.*

Restate the sentence twice, using each subject individually. Bob will be going. I will be going. "Me will be going" does not make sense.

When a pronoun is immediately followed by a noun (as in "we boys"), say the sentence without the added noun. Your ear will tell you the correct pronoun form.

Example: *(We/Us) boys played football last year.*

Restate the sentence twice, without the noun. We played football last year. Us played football last year. Clearly "We played football last year" makes more sense.

# Using Commas

## FLOW

Commas break the flow of text. To test whether they are necessary, read the text to yourself and pause for a moment at each comma. If the pauses seem natural, then the commas are correct. If they are not, then the commas are not correct.

## NONESSENTIAL CLAUSES AND PHRASES

A comma should be used to set off **nonessential** clauses and participial phrases from the rest of the sentence. To determine if a clause is **essential**, remove it from the sentence. If the removal of the clause would alter the meaning of the sentence, then it is essential. Otherwise, it is nonessential.

Example: *John Smith, who was a disciple of Andrew Collins, was a noted archeologist.*

In the example above, the sentence describes John Smith's fame in archeology. The fact that he was a disciple of Andrew Collins is not necessary to that meaning. Therefore, separating it from the rest of the sentence with commas is correct.

Do not use a comma if the clause or phrase is essential to the meaning of the sentence.

Example: *Anyone who appreciates obscure French poetry will enjoy reading the book.*

If the phrase "who appreciates obscure French poetry" is removed, the sentence indicates that anyone would enjoy reading the book, not just those with an appreciation for obscure French poetry. However, the sentence implies that the book's enjoyment may not be for everyone, so the phrase is essential.

Another, perhaps easier, way to determine if the clause is essential is to see if it has a comma at its beginning or end. Consistent, parallel punctuation must be used, and so if you can determine a comma exists at one side of the clause, then you can be certain that a comma should exist on the opposite side.

## INDEPENDENT CLAUSES

Use a comma before the words *and, but, or, nor, for,* or *yet* when they join independent clauses. To determine if two clauses are independent, remove the word that joins them. If each clause can stand alone as a complete sentence, then they are independent and need a comma between them.

Example: *He ran down the street, and then he ran over the bridge.*

He ran down the street. Then he ran over the bridge. Both clauses are capable of being their own sentence. Therefore, a comma must be used along with the word "and" to join the two clauses together.

If one or more of the clauses would be a fragment if left alone, then it must be joined to another clause and a comma is not needed between them.

Example: *He ran down the street and over the bridge.*

He ran down the street. Over the bridge. "Over the bridge" is a sentence fragment and cannot stand alone. No comma is necessary to join it with "He ran down the street." Note that this does not cover the use of "and" when separating items in a series, such as "red, white, and blue." In these cases a comma is not always necessary between the last two items in the series, but in general it is best to use one.

## PARENTHETICAL EXPRESSIONS

Commas should separate parenthetical expressions such as the following: *after all, by the way, for example, in fact,* and *on the other hand.*

Example: *By the way, she is in my biology class.*

If the parenthetical expression is in the middle of the sentence, a comma is placed both before and after it.

Example: *She is, after all, in my biology class.*

However, these expressions are not always used parenthetically, so commas may not be necessary. To determine if an expression is parenthetical, see if you need to pause when you read the sentence. If you do, then it is parenthetical and needs commas.

Example: *You can tell by the way she plays the violin that she enjoys its music.*

No pause is necessary in reading that example sentence. Therefore, the phrase "by the way" does not need commas around it.

## HYPHENS

Hyphenate a **compound adjective** that is directly before the noun it describes.

Example 1: He was the best-known kid in the school.
Example 2: The shot came from that grass-covered hill.
Example 3: The well-drained fields were dry soon after the rain.

## USE YOUR EAR

Read each sentence carefully, inserting the answer choices in the blanks. Don't stop at the first answer choice if you think it is right, but read them all. What may seem like the best choice at first may not be after you have had time to read all of the choices. Allow your ear to determine what **sounds right**. Often one or two answer choices can be immediately ruled out because they don't sound logical or make sense.

## CONTEXTUAL CLUES

It bears repeating that contextual clues offer a lot of help in determining the best answer. Key words in the sentence will allow you to determine exactly which answer choice is the best replacement text.

Example:

*Archeology has shown that some of the ruins of the ancient city of Babylon are approximately 500 years _____ Mesopotamian predecessors.*

    a. as old as any supposed
    b. as old as their supposed
    c. older than their supposed
    d. older than a supposed

In this example, the **key word** "supposed" is used. Archaeology would either confirm that the predecessors to Babylon were more ancient or disprove that supposition. Since supposed was used, it would imply that archaeology had disproved the accepted belief, making Babylon actually older, not as old as, so either answer choice C or D is correct.

Since choice D contains the word "a," this would be correct if "predecessors" was singular. Since "predecessors" is plural (with an "s" on the end), choice C must be correct.

Furthermore, because "500 years" is used, answer choices A and B can be ruled out. Years are used to show either absolute or relative age. If two objects are as old as each other, no years are necessary to describe that relationship, and it would be sufficient to say, "The ancient city of Babylon is approximately as old as their supposed Mesopotamian predecessors," without using the term "500 years."

## SIMPLICITY IS BEST

Simplicity cannot be overstated. You should never choose a longer, more complicated, or wordier replacement if a simple one will do. When a point can be made with fewer words, choose that answer. However, do not sacrifice the flow of text for simplicity. If an answer is simple, but does not make sense, then it is not correct.

Beware of **added phrases** that don't add anything of meaning, such as "to be" or "as to them." Often these added phrases will occur just before a colon, which may indicate a list of items. However, the colon does not need a lengthy introduction.

The phrases "of which [...] are" in the below examples are wordy and unnecessary. They should be removed and the colon placed directly after the words "sport" and "following".

Example 1: *There are many advantages to running as a sport, of which the top advantages are:*

Example 2: *The school supplies necessary were the following, of which a few are:*

## DON'T PANIC

Panicking will not put down any more words on paper. Therefore, it isn't helpful. When you first see the topic, if your mind goes blank, take a deep breath. Force yourself to mechanically go through the steps listed earlier.

Secondly, don't get clock fever. It's easy to be overwhelmed when you're looking at a page that is mostly blank, your mind is full of random, confused thoughts, and the clock is ticking down faster than you would like. But you brainstormed first so you don't have to keep coming up with ideas. If you're running out of time and you have a lot of ideas you haven't covered, don't be afraid to make some cuts. Start picking the best of the remaining ideas and expand on those few. Don't feel like you have to write down and expand all of your ideas.

## CHECK YOUR WORK

It is more important to have a shorter paper that is well written and well organized than a longer paper that is poorly written and poorly organized. Don't keep writing about a subject just to add words and sentences, and certainly don't start repeating yourself. Expand on the ideas that you identified in the brainstorming session and make sure that you save a few minutes at the end to review.

Leave time at the end, at least a few minutes, to go back and **check over your work**. Reread and make sure that everything you've written makes sense and flows well. Clean up any spelling or grammar mistakes that you might have made.

As you proofread, make sure there aren't any sentence fragments or run-ons. Check for sentences that are too short or too long. If the sentence is too short, check to see if you have an identifiable subject and verb. If it is too long, break it up into two separate sentences. Watch out for any "big" words you may have used. It's good to use difficult vocabulary words, but only if you are positive that you are using them correctly. Your paper has to be correct, but it doesn't have to be fancy. You're not trying to impress anyone with your vocabulary, but with your ability to develop and express ideas.

# Summary

Depending on your test-taking preferences and personality, the writing will probably be your hardest or your easiest section. You are required to go through the entire process of writing a paper in a brief amount of time, which can be quite a challenge.

Focus on each of the steps listed above. Go through the process of creative flow first, generating ideas and thoughts about the topic. Then organize those ideas into a smooth, logical flow. Pick out the best ideas from your list. Decide which main idea or angle of the topic you will discuss.

Create a recognizable structure in your paper, with an introductory paragraph explaining what you have decided on and what your main points will be. Use the body paragraphs to expand on those main points and have a conclusion that wraps up the issue or topic.

Save a few moments to go back and review what you have written. Clean up any minor mistakes and give it those last few critical touches that can make a huge difference. Finally, be proud and confident of what you have written!

# TOEFL Practice Test

## Reading

### TEST FORMAT CHANGES

As of August 2019, the TOEFL iBT reading section was reduced to 10 questions per passage and a time limit of 54-72 minutes total. The question types and number of passages have not changed with this modification. Despite TOEFL's changes, we have included the full length of the test to help you to practice as much as possible.

### ADDITIONAL INSTRUCTIONS FOR THE TEST

When you take the real test, you will be given a university-level text. After fully reading the text, you will be able to access the questions. During this time, you will be able to refer back to the passage while answering the questions. You will have three to four reading passages during your test and twenty minutes to spend on each passage. Take your time and remember that all of the answers can be found in the passage.

### PASSAGE 1

*Questions 1–14 are based on the following passage.*

In 1603, Queen Elizabeth I of England died. She had never married and had no heir, so the throne passed to a distant relative: James Stuart, the son of Elizabeth's cousin and one-time rival for the throne, Mary, Queen of Scots. James was crowned King James I of England. At the time, he was also King James VI of Scotland, and the combination of roles would create a spirit of conflict that haunted the two nations for generations to come.

The conflict developed as a result of rising tensions among the people within the nations, as well as between them. Scholars in the 21st century are far too hasty in dismissing the role of religion in political disputes, but religion undoubtedly played a role in the problems that faced England and Scotland. By the time of James Stuart's succession to the English throne, the English people had firmly embraced the teachings of Protestant theology. Similarly, the Scottish Lowlands was decisively Protestant. In the Scottish Highlands, however, the clans retained their Catholic faith. James acknowledged the Church of England and sanctioned the largely Protestant translation of the Bible that still bears his name.

James's son King Charles I proved himself to be less committed to the Protestant Church of England. Charles married the Catholic Princess Henrietta Maria of France, and there were suspicions among the English and the Lowland Scots that Charles was quietly a Catholic. Charles's own political troubles extended beyond religion in this case, and he was beheaded in 1649. Eventually, his son King Charles II would be crowned, and this Charles is believed to have converted secretly to the Catholic Church. Charles II died without a legitimate heir, and his brother James ascended to the throne as King James II.

James was recognized to be a practicing Catholic, and his commitment to Catholicism would prove to be his downfall. James's wife Mary Beatrice lost a number of children during their infancy, and when she became pregnant again in 1687 the public became concerned. If James had a son, that son would undoubtedly be raised a Catholic, and the English people would not stand for this. Mary gave birth to a son, but the story quickly circulated that the royal child had died and the child named James's heir was a foundling smuggled in. James, his

51

wife, and his infant son were forced to flee; and James's Protestant daughter Mary was crowned the queen.

In spite of a strong resemblance to the king, the young James was generally rejected among the English and the Lowland Scots, who referred to him as "the Pretender." But in the Highlands the Catholic princeling was welcomed. He inspired a group known as *Jacobites*, to reflect the Latin version of his name. His own son Charles, known affectionately as Bonnie Prince Charlie, would eventually raise an army and attempt to recapture what he believed to be his throne. The movement was soundly defeated at the Battle of Culloden in 1746, and England and Scotland have remained Protestant ever since.

**1. Which of the following sentences contains an opinion on the part of the author?**

a. James was recognized to be a practicing Catholic, and his commitment to Catholicism would prove to be his downfall.
b. James' son King Charles I proved himself to be less committed to the Protestant Church of England.
c. The movement was soundly defeated at the Battle of Culloden in 1746, and England and Scotland have remained Protestant ever since.
d. Scholars in the 21st century are far too hasty in dismissing the role of religion in political disputes, but religion undoubtedly played a role in the problems that faced England and Scotland.

**2. Which of the following is a logical conclusion based on the information that is provided within the passage?**

a. Like Elizabeth I, Charles II never married and thus never had children.
b. The English people were relieved each time that James II's wife Mary lost another child, as this prevented the chance of a Catholic monarch.
c. Charles I's beheading had less to do with religion than with other political problems that England was facing.
d. Unlike his son and grandsons, King James I had no Catholic leanings and was a faithful follower of the Protestant Church of England.

**3. Based on the information that is provided within the passage, which of the following can be inferred about King James II's son?**

a. Considering his resemblance to King James II, the young James was very likely the legitimate child of the king and the queen.
b. Given the queen's previous inability to produce a healthy child, the English and the Lowland Scots were right in suspecting the legitimacy of the prince.
c. James "the Pretender" was not as popular among the Highland clans as his son Bonnie Prince Charlie.
d. James was unable to acquire the resources needed to build the army and plan the invasion that his son succeeded in doing.

**4. Which of the following best describes the organization of the information in the passage?**

a. Cause-effect
b. Chronological sequence
c. Problem-solution
d. Comparison-contrast

**5. Which of the following best describes the author's intent in the passage?**

    a. To persuade
    b. To entertain
    c. To express feeling
    d. To inform

**6. What can be inferred from paragraph two about the author's view of 21st century scholars?**

    a. 21st century scholars often disregard the role of religious views in historical political disputes.
    b. 21st century scholars make hasty observations about historical political disputes.
    c. 21st century scholars lack the details necessary to understand historical political disputes.
    d. 21st century scholars think that religion is never used in political disputes.

**7. What is the nickname of the founder of a group called the *Jacobites*?**

    a. Jacob
    b. The Deceiver
    c. The Pretender
    d. The Fool

**8. Who does the passage say ascended the throne because someone else did not have a legitimate heir?**

    a. King James Stuart
    b. Queen Elizabeth I
    c. King Charles II
    d. King James II

**9. Which of the following best describes what the passage is about?**

    a. The lineage of the current Queen of England
    b. The history of religions in Scotland and in England
    c. The role of religion in conflict between England and Scotland
    d. The history and origin of the Jacobites

**10. What was the result of King Charles I's political troubles?**

    a. He was beheaded
    b. He was exiled
    c. He was hanged
    d. He was dethroned

**11. Based on the following sentence, what can you infer about the meaning of the italicized word? Mary gave birth to a son, but the story quickly circulated that the royal child had died and the child named James's heir was a *foundling* smuggled in.**

    a. A prince
    b. An orphan
    c. A nephew
    d. An illegitimate child

## 12. What kind of tone does this passage have?

a. Humorous
b. Informative
c. Solemn
d. Sarcastic

## 13. Which piece of information is least important to the purpose of the passage?

a. Queen Elizabeth I died in 1603.
b. King James I had a Bible translation commissioned.
c. Bonnie Prince Charlie attempted to reclaim the throne.
d. King Charles II was believed to have secretly converted to Catholicism.

## 14. What was the end result of the conflict after the Battle of Culloden?

a. England and Scotland became Catholic as a result of the battle.
b. James the Pretender and his wife had to flee for safety.
c. This battle started conflict that would continue for generations.
d. England and Scotland have remained Protestant.

## PASSAGE 2

*Questions 15–28 are based on the following passage.*

Stories have been a part of the world since the beginning of recorded time. For millennia before the invention of the printing press, stories of the world were passed down throughout the generations through oral tradition. With the invention of the printing press, which made written material available to wide ranges of audiences, books were mass-produced and introduced into greater society. Before the printing press was invented, books had to be hand copied, which made them very difficult to make and very costly as a result.

For the last several centuries, books have been at the forefront of education and entertainment. With the invention of the Internet, reliance on books for information quickly changed. Soon, almost everything that anyone needed to know could be accessed through the Internet. Large printed volumes of encyclopedias became unnecessary as all of the information was easily available on the Internet.

Despite the progression of the Internet, printed media was still very popular in the forms of both fiction and nonfiction books. Similarly, newspapers are a format of reading material that have been widespread in availability and use. While waiting for an appointment, enduring a several-hour flight, or relaxing before sleep, books, magazines, and newspapers have been a reliable and convenient source of entertainment, and one that society has not been willing to give up.

With the progression and extreme convenience of technology, printed books will soon become a thing of the past. Inventions such as the iPad from Macintosh and the Kindle have made the need for any kind of printed media unnecessary. With a rechargeable battery, a large screen, and the ability to have several books saved on file, electronic options will soon take over and society will no longer see printed books.

Some people still cling to the old format of printed books as they enjoy owning and reading from paper materials. Although some people may say that the act of reading is not complete without turning a page, sliding a finger across the screen or pressing a button to read more on the next page is just as satisfying to the reader. The iPad and Kindle are devices

54

that have qualities similar to a computer and can be used for so much more than just reading. These devices are therefore better than books because they have multiple uses.

In a cultural society that is part of the world, and due to a longstanding tradition, stories will always be an important way to communicate ideas and provide information and entertainment. Centuries ago, stories could only be remembered and retold through speech. Printed media changed the way the world communicated and was connected, and now, as we move forward with technology, it is only a matter of time before we must say goodbye to the printed past and welcome the digital and electronic future.

**15. What is the main argument of this essay?**

a. The iPad and Kindle are easier to read than books.
b. The printing press was a great invention.
c. The Internet is how people receive information.
d. Technology will soon replace printed material.

**16. What is the main purpose of paragraph 1?**

a. To explain oral tradition
b. To explain the importance of the printing press
c. To explain the progression of stories within society
d. To introduce the essay

**17. According to the essay, what was the first way that stories were communicated and passed down?**

a. Oral tradition
b. Printed books
c. Technology
d. Hand writing

**18. Which of the following statements is an opinion?**

a. Despite the progression of the Internet, printed media was still very popular in the forms of both fiction and nonfiction books.
b. Although some people may say that the act of reading is not complete without turning a page, sliding a finger across the screen or pressing a button to read more on the next page is just as satisfying to the reader.
c. With the invention of the Internet, reliance on books for information quickly changed.
d. Stories have been a part of the world since the beginning of recorded time.

**19. What is a secondary argument the author makes?**

a. Devices such as the iPad or Kindle are better than books because they have multiple uses.
b. Books are still important to have while waiting for an appointment or taking a flight.
c. Printed encyclopedias are still used and more convenient that using the Internet.
d. With technology, there will soon be no need for stories.

**20. What is the author's purpose in writing this essay?**

a. To inform the reader about the history of stories
b. To persuade the reader about the merits of digital media
c. To tell the reader an entertaining story
d. To inform the reader about different types of print media

**21. What kind of phrasing indicates the author's purpose?**

    a. The author states information in an unbiased way.
    b. The author tells an entertaining story.
    c. The author presents his information in a historical and factual manner.
    d. The author asserts that one option is better than another.

**22. What is the main reason the author gives for saying that books are going out of use?**

    a. Books are too costly to print.
    b. Digital media is more convenient.
    c. Storytellers prefer to keep an oral tradition alive.
    d. People do not like to read as much.

**23. Which of the following was not a reliable and convenient use that the author presents for books?**

    a. Relaxing before sleep
    b. Waiting for an appointment
    c. Studying for a test
    d. Enduring a several-hour flight

**24. How does the author feel about the change in types of media for storytelling?**

    a. The author wants to go back to the oral tradition.
    b. The author embraces change and looks forward to digital print.
    c. The author is uncertain about the change.
    d. The author likes paper books and does not want the way it is to change.

**25. What would be a strong title for this passage?**

    a. Stories and How to Tell Them
    b. Story-Telling and Technology
    c. The Digital Future of Reading
    d. A History of Print Media

**26. The author gives several reasons that electronic devices will help make printed books unnecessary. Which of the following is not mentioned in the passage?**

    a. A large screen
    b. The ability to have several books saved on file
    c. Rechargeable
    d. Being able to listen to audiobooks

**27. Which best represents the organization of the information in the passage?**

    a. Problem-solution
    b. Cause-effect
    c. Chronological sequence
    d. Comparison-contrast

**28. According to the author, some people may say that the act of reading is:**

    a. Not complete without turning a page.
    b. Not complete without the smell of a book.
    c. Not complete without being able to highlight information.
    d. Not complete without sliding a finger across the screen.

## PASSAGE 3

*Questions 29–42 are based on the following passage.*

### "So That Nobody Has To Go To School If They Don't Want To"

*An Excerpt by Roger Sipher*

A decline in standardized test scores is but the most recent indicator that American education is in trouble. One reason for the crisis is that present mandatory-attendance laws force many to attend school who have no wish to be there. Such children have little desire to learn and are so antagonistic to school that neither they nor more highly motivated students receive the quality education that is the birthright of every American. The solution to this problem is simple: Abolish compulsory-attendance laws and allow only those who are committed to getting an education to attend.

Most parents want a high school education for their children. Unfortunately, compulsory attendance hampers the ability of public school officials to enforce legitimate educational and disciplinary policies and thereby make the education a good one. Private schools have no such problem. They can fail or dismiss students, knowing such students can attend public school. Without compulsory attendance, public schools would be freer to oust students whose academic or personal behavior undermines the educational mission of the institution.

Abolition of archaic attendance laws would produce enormous dividends:

- First, it would alert everyone that school is a serious place where one goes to learn. Schools are neither day-care centers nor indoor street corners. Young people who resist learning should stay away; indeed, an end to compulsory schooling would require them to stay away.
- Second, students opposed to learning would not be able to pollute the educational atmosphere for those who want to learn. Teachers could stop policing recalcitrant students and start educating.
- Third, grades would show what they are supposed to: how well a student is learning. Parents could again read report cards and know if their children were making progress.
- Fourth, public esteem for schools would increase. People would stop regarding them as way stations for adolescents and start thinking of them as institutions for educating America's youth.
- Fifth, elementary schools would change because students would find out early they had better learn something or risk flunking out later. Elementary teachers would no longer have to pass their failures on to junior high and high school.
- Sixth, the cost of enforcing compulsory education would be eliminated. Despite enforcement efforts, nearly 15 percent of the school-age children in our largest cities are almost permanently absent from school.

Communities could use these savings to support institutions to deal with young people not in school. If, in the long run, these institutions prove more costly, at least we would not confuse their mission with that of schools. Schools should be for education. At present, they are only tangentially so. They have attempted to serve an all-encompassing social function, trying to be all things to all people. In the process they have failed miserably at what they were originally formed to accomplish.

**29. What is the main purpose for this passage?**

a. To report on students who do not want to go to school
b. To discuss a variety of policies regarding school attendance
c. To give reasons for the decline in standardized test scores in America
d. To convince the reader that school attendance should not be mandatory

**30. Based on the context of paragraph one, what could be a synonym for the word _compulsory_?**

a. Decisive
b. Required
c. Optional
d. Frequent

**31. What can you infer to be the author's view of modern educational policies?**

a. The author is indifferent to current policies.
b. The author is satisfied with current policies.
c. The author is against the current policies.
d. The author is confused about the current policies.

**32. Which of the following best sums up the passage?**

a. Standardized test scores are in decline and a change of policy would improve conditions.
b. Schools do not teach and are currently used more as a social function instead of for education.
c. Parents want an education for their children but are unable to get their children to behave.
d. Communities need to save money to support better educational institutions.

**33. Based on the context of paragraph three, what seems like the best synonym for the word _archaic_?**

a. Out-dated
b. Vanishing
c. Expensive
d. Weak

**34. According to the passage, why do private schools not encounter the same problems as public schools?**

a. The students at private schools are better.
b. Private school teachers are higher quality.
c. Private schools are able to fail or dismiss students.
d. Private schools do not require their students to attend classes.

**35. Which of the following is not a reason the author gives as a benefit for ending required attendance?**

a. Public esteem for schools would increase.
b. Student transportation costs would decrease.
c. Cost of enforcement would decrease.
d. Grades would become more effective.

**36. Based on the context in the final paragraph, what could be a synonym for the word** *tangentially*?

    a. Expensively
    b. Confusingly
    c. Fully
    d. Slightly

**37. Which of the following would be a strong concluding sentence?**

    a. New attendance policies hold the power to improve test scores and make schools great again.
    b. With these changes, parents can ensure that the needs of their children are met.
    c. Parents should be responsible for ensuring that their children go to school, rather than the government.
    d. Through abolishing these outdated policies, schools can become all that they were meant to be.

**38. How does the passage suggest that students who do not want to be at school undermine the mission of educational institutions?**

    a. Schools are only interested in teaching those who want to learn.
    b. Students who do not want to come to class are more aggressive and bully others.
    c. Students who do not want to attend classes have harmful effects on other students.
    d. Schools strive to have the highest attendance rates possible and those who do not want to be in school do not always attend.

**39. What does the author mean in using the word** *birthright* **to refer to American education?**

    a. Americans are expected to be able to receive a quality education.
    b. Americans are literally entitled to education as an inheritance.
    c. By being born in America, one has a higher chance at becoming educated.
    d. Americans are expected to be educated as opposed to other nationalities.

**40. Based on the context of paragraph three, what could be a synonym for the word** *recalcitrant*?

    a. Nervous
    b. Lazy
    c. Unruly
    d. Sleepy

**41. How does the title relate to the passage?**

    a. The title directly relates to the passage, insinuating that school is not fun and should only be attended when a student wants to.
    b. The title is satiric and mocks the notion that laws require students to attend school even if they do not want to.
    c. The title is sarcastic and opposes the true meaning, that all students should go to school.
    d. The title insinuates that students should be surveyed to find out which students actually want to attend school.

**42. How does the author suggest that attendance law reform would help with grades?**

    a. Grades would improve because of a lack of distractions.

    b. Grades would start to match student performance.

    c. All students would begin passing their tests.

    d. Student grades would stay about the same because teachers would use harder tests.

# Listening

## TEST FORMAT CHANGES

As of August 2019, the TOEFL iBT listening section was reduced to 3-4 lectures with 6 questions per lecture and a time limit of 41-57 minutes total. The question types have not changed with this modification. Despite TOEFL's changes, we have included the full length of the test to help you to practice as much as possible.

## ADDITIONAL INSTRUCTIONS FOR THE TEST

There are two types of listening samples in the listening portion of the TOEFL: short lectures and conversations. There are four to six short lectures and two to three conversations, each ranging from three to five minutes long. When you take the real test, you will first see a photo that should help orient you to the material, followed by an audio clip of either a conversation or a lecture. While the audio is playing, you should take notes. Try to identify main points if possible. After listening to the audio clip, you will be given five to six multiple choice questions. **You will not be given a transcript or be allowed to listen to the recording again.** A transcript of each conversation and lecture is included for your reference after the answer explanations.

**Listening Passage 1: A conversation between a male student and a female student**

> **Practice Audio: <u>Listening Passage 1: Conversation</u>**
> Visit mometrix.com/academy and enter Code: 407056

Questions:

**1. What was Claudia upset about?**

  a. The status of a group project for her philosophy class
  b. A difficult project designing a bridge for her engineering class
  c. Her difficulty in understanding Aristotle's philosophies and influences
  d. Receiving a poor grade on her midterm exams

**2. What were the components of the group project assignment? Mark the two correct choices.**

  a. A 10-page paper
  b. A 20-page paper
  c. A 20-minute presentation
  d. A 10-minute presentation

**3. In Claudia's sentence: "Thanks for commiserating with me, Miguel," the word *commiserating* most nearly means which of the following?**

  a. Communicating
  b. Correcting
  c. Agreeing
  d. Sympathizing

**4. Why does Claudia think her group is not taking the project seriously? Select two answers.**

  a. Because one student does not enjoy philosophy class
  b. Because one student did a poor job covering his material
  c. Because two group members have not yet started on the project
  d. Because they know the project will not impact their grade

61

**5. Read the following statement from the conversation and then answer the question:**

*Male student: I had to carry the weight of the whole group since no one held up their end.*

What does the male student mean when he says he "had to carry the weight of the whole group"?

    a. His bridge design had to hold the entire load dictated by the assignment.
    b. He needed to manage everyone in his group and assign them various roles in the project.
    c. He had to take on the bulk of the group work by himself.
    d. He had to demonstrate how much weight the bridge could hold before it collapsed.

**6. Why does the female student say: "Before this, I always loved group projects, but now, my opinion has shifted"?**

    a. She used to enjoy group projects, but after the current negative experience, she no longer likes them.
    b. She didn't used to like group projects, but after the current negative experience, she now enjoys them.
    c. She has changed her views of things after learning about the ideals of notable philosophers.
    d. She didn't used to like philosophy class, but after this project, she now enjoys it.

**Listening Passage 2: A lecture by a male professor**

> **Practice Audio: <u>Listening Passage 2: Lecture</u>**
> Visit mometrix.com/academy and enter Code: 517190

Questions:

**7. What is the main topic of the lecture?**

    a. The range of developmental disorders that future teachers should be aware of
    b. The varied ways in which Sensory Processing Disorder presents itself
    c. The cures for Sensory Processing Disorder
    d. How to teach students who are interested in education and children

**8. Based on the information the professor shares in the lecture, why are there sensory integration issues for someone with SPD?**

    a. Because people with SPD respond well to occupational therapy, or OT
    b. Because the various senses of the body are interrelated and do not occur in isolation
    c. Because someone with SPD and is always both a sensory seeker for some senses and sensory defensive for others
    d. Because Sensory Processing Disorder used to be called Sensory Integration Disorder

**9. Why does the professor explain in detail about the presentation of SPD?**

    a. Because many of the students listening to the lecture want to become teachers so they will need to be aware of its varied presentations in students
    b. Because many of the students listening to the lecture have Sensory Processing Disorder so they should learn more about it
    c. Because many of the students listening to the lecture want to become doctors who will diagnose the condition so they need to understand the warning signs
    d. Because SPD has a very straightforward presentation so it's easier to discuss and identify compared to other learning disabilities like ADHD

**10. According to the lecture, which of the following would be considered "comorbidities"?**

a. Sensory Processing Disorder and autism
b. Touch and hearing
c. Sensory Processing Disorder and Occupational Therapy
d. Occupational Therapy and classroom accommodations

**11. Why doesn't the professor cover the specific OT interventions and classroom modifications for students with SPD in this lecture?**

a. Because there are no helpful OT treatments or classroom accommodations since SPD is so varied
b. Because the students listening to the lecture aren't interested in learning about OT interventions and classroom modifications
c. Because there is no time left in the class
d. Because the textbook covers this material well so it will be assigned for homework

**12. According to the lecture, what are the two primary types of SPD?**

a. Sensory-seeking and sensory-defensive
b. Sensory integration and sensory processing
c. The five senses and interoception
d. OT and learning disabilities

**13. Based on the information in the lecture, which of the following would someone with Sensory Processing Disorder likely struggle with?**

a. Remembering to stop and smell the roses
b. Chewing food enough to prevent choking
c. Reading a book in a noisy classroom
d. Differentiating various colors

**Listening Passage 3: A lecture by a female professor**

> **Practice Audio: Listening Passage 3: Lecture**
> Visit mometrix.com/academy and enter Code: 535116

Questions:

**14. What was the main topic addressed in the lecture?**

a. The differences in Theravada and Mahayana Buddhism
b. The difference between Indian and Chinese religions
c. The different ways that meditation is used in Buddhism
d. The importance of any religion to appeal to the masses

**15. According to the professor, what is the primary difference between Theravada and Mahayana Buddhism?**

a. Theravada is Indian and Mahayana is Chinese.
b. Theravada was only accessible to the upper classes while Mahayana was designed to be accessible to the masses.
c. Theravada was designed after Mahayana Buddhism.
d. Theravada Buddhists were discouraged from meditating while Mahayana Buddhists stressed the importance of daily meditation.

16. **What does the professor mean when she says, "We've only just started to scratch the surface here"?**

   a. We are out of time today.
   b. We have covered the necessary material.
   c. We have just begun exploring this material.
   d. We have just created a little damage so the material is still usable.

17. **What does the professor imply about the evolution of Buddhism in China?**

   a. That there is a very clear, simple, and linear path to its evolution
   b. That disagreements in fundamental concepts spawned the emergence of new sects
   c. That it was easily adapted from Indian culture to Chinese because of the striking similarities
   d. That a consensus vote was frequently used to shape the future direction of the religion at large

18. **Which of the following are components of Theravada? Pick two answers.**

   a. The Four Noble Truths
   b. The eightfold path
   c. Increased accessibility
   d. Being a "Lesser Vehicle"

19. **Read the following statement from the conversation and then answer the question:**

   *This made Theravada Buddhism an esoteric religion because the people of the lower and middle classes were unable to devote so much time to meditation.*

   **What does the word *esoteric* most nearly mean?**

   a. Confusing or irrational
   b. Expensive and hard to afford
   c. Accessible and easily understood by all
   d. Obscure or reserved for only certain people

   **Listening Passage 4: A lecture by a male professor, with interaction from students**

   **Practice Audio: Listening Passage 4: Lecture and Discussion**
   Visit mometrix.com/academy and enter Code: 843665

Questions:

20. **A geology student is weighing rock samples. The true weight of the rock is 12.0 grams. The student weighs it on his new scale three times and obtains the weights of 8.0 grams, 8.2 grams, and 8.1 grams. How would you describe his results?**

   a. Both accurate and precise
   b. Neither accurate nor precise
   c. Accurate but not precise
   d. Precise but not accurate

**21. Based on the information in the lecture and discussion, in a research study, a person's gender would be measured on what scale?**

    a. Nominal
    b. Ordinal
    c. Interval
    d. Ratio

**22. What does the professor mean when he says, "You hit the nail on the head"?**

    a. You're working hard.
    b. You're using the right tool.
    c. Your answer is correct.
    d. Good effort but you're wrong.

**23. In what situation would the students in the class be most likely to use the information from the lecture?**

    a. During archery or shooting targets
    b. Conducting research studies or experiments
    c. When weighing things in a lab
    d. When taking an exam in history class

**24. In what way was the lecture organized to discuss the four measurement scales?**

    a. In order of importance
    b. In cause and effect order
    c. In chronological order
    d. In order of increasing specificity

**25. Read the following statement from the conversation and then answer the question:**

*Male student's response: Interval scales are essentially an intermediary between the lack of specificity of nominal and ordinal but a little less defined than ratio with no absolute zero, so I think we cannot be quite as precise as ratio but more than the lower levels of measurement.*

**Which of the following is the best way to paraphrase his statement?**

    a. Interval scale measurements are more specific and thus more precise than nominal and ordinal scales but less precise than ratio scales because they lack an absolute zero.
    b. Interval scale measurements are less specific and thus less precise than nominal and ordinal scales but more precise than ratio scales because they lack an absolute zero.
    c. Interval scales are better than ratio and ordinal scales.
    d. Interval scales are the most specific and precise scales.

**Listening Passage 5: A conversation between a female professor and a male student**

> **Practice Audio: <u>Listening Passage 5: Conversation</u>**
> Visit mometrix.com/academy and enter Code: 474952

Questions:

**26. What is the main problem the student is having?**

a. He wants to become a chemistry tutor.
b. He cannot find time to make it to office hours.
c. He is struggling to understand the chemistry material.
d. He does not know where the Student Resource Center is.

**27. According to the conversation, which of the following are ways that Connor can receive help? Select three answers.**

a. Office hours with his professor
b. Reviewing his textbook
c. Receiving assistance on his exam
d. Getting tutoring at the Student Resource Center
e. Study reference materials in the library

**28. When would be the best time for Connor to meet with his professor?**

a. Tuesdays and Thursdays after trigonometry class, during office hours
b. Any time the Student Resource Center is open
c. Any day besides Tuesday and Thursday because he has trigonometry class
d. Whenever his pride is in the way

**29. Which of the following are true about the Student Resource Center? Select two answers.**

a. It's on the second floor of the library.
b. You need a referral.
c. There are only science tutors.
d. It's free for graduate students.

**30. What is meant by Connor's statement: "Availability wasn't the limiting factor; I think it was my pride."**

a. I honestly felt proud about how I performed on the exam.
b. I honestly wasn't too busy; I think I just didn't want to admit that I needed help.
c. I honestly am not really busy but I wanted to make you proud.
d. There is a limit to how much time I can spend on this and still be proud of myself.

**31. Based on the conversation, why did Connor not use the textbook to study?**

a. He has not purchased it yet.
b. He wasn't aware that he didn't understand the material.
c. He didn't know the textbook covered the material.
d. He found the writing to be dense and the examples were confusing.

**Listening Passage 6: A lecture by a female professor**

**Practice Audio: Listening Passage 6: Lecture**
Visit mometrix.com/academy and enter Code: 756602

Questions:

**32. What was the main topic of the lecture?**

a. The importance of Shakespeare's plays
b. The complicated psychology of Lady Macbeth
c. The murder Macbeth committed
d. The reasons that people are manipulative

**33. What does the professor mean when she says, "I can see I'm losing some of you..."?**

a. Her students do not agree with her argument.
b. Her students are dropping her course because it is too challenging.
c. Her students are about to graduate .
d. Her students are losing focus because they are worried about their exams.

**34. Why might the professor say, "Do you guys see how the key to Lady Macbeth's strategy for gaining influence over her husband is to somewhat switch the gender roles within her marriage?" without pausing to call on her students for responses?**

a. To help students stay focused and not get off topic answering questions
b. To encourage students to be critical thinkers as she strengthens her argument
c. To dominate the conversation and prevent interruptions
d. To remind the students that they have a lot to learn

**35. What does the professor argue is a strength of Shakespeare's plays and a quality that makes him a successful playwright in history?**

a. The fact that people have read his plays for centuries and his works are well-preserved
b. That his works consider the complexities of human nature through character development
c. The fact that he persuades audience members to be deviant
d. The fact that his works teach readers about people and places from a vibrant period in history

**36. The professor would likely describe Lady Macbeth as which of the following?**

a. A very "good" and loyal wife
b. A very "evil" and manipulative wife
c. A character who is realistic in her psychological complexities
d. A predictable and mundane character

# Speaking

## TEST FORMAT CHANGES

As of August 2019, the TOEFL iBT speaking section was reduced to 4 speaking tasks and a time limit of 17 minutes total. The question types have not changed with this modification. Despite TOEFL's changes, we have included the full length of the test to help you to practice as much as possible.

## ADDITIONAL INSTRUCTIONS FOR THE TEST

When you take the real test, you will have a variety of tasks to complete for the speaking section. In the independent speaking tasks, you will answer questions about familiar topics. You will have 15 seconds to prepare and will have to provide a 45 second response in answering the question. These are common conversation types that you should practice in English as much as possible prior to your test.

The three integrated tasks will require you to read either read a short text, listen to a short lecture, or listen to a conversation prior to responding. You will have 30 seconds to prepare for the lecture responses and short text responses. For the conversational section, you will have 20 seconds to prepare. In each task, you will have 60 seconds to provide a response to the question.

### Prompts

**1. What do you think your life will be like in ten years? Describe what you think you'll be doing and where you'd like to be, and explain why.**

> Preparation Time: 15 seconds
> Response Time: 45 seconds

**2. Some people prefer classes that meet once a week in a single long session while others prefer courses that meet several days per week for a shorter duration. What is your opinion? Explain why.**

> Preparation Time: 15 seconds
> Response Time: 45 seconds

## 3. Read the following passage and then listen to the conversation. Lastly, answer the question that follows them.

*The following text was reported by the University administrators to all students and their parents. Read the announcement. (The allotted reading time on the exam would be 45-60 seconds).*

### ANNOUNCEMENT:

The University Public Safety and Parking Services Department has decided that, effective at the start of the upcoming academic year, only juniors and seniors will be eligible to purchase campus parking permits. While there have been a limited number of available permits for underclassmen over the past few years, the Public Services department and University administration agree that reverting back to the junior- and senior-only policy is in the best interest of our campus community. This decision comes with considerable deliberation and a majority vote. It was determined that the limitation of available spaces and resultant permit fee posed a prohibitive cost for many of our students. Additionally, we believe that reserving the privilege of on-campus vehicles for just juniors and seniors will eliminate the need for the extensive application and lottery process. All interested upperclassmen will now simply register their vehicle online and pay a nominal parking permit fee. Lastly, we hope this decision will strengthen our campus community by encouraging freshmen to stay on campus and engage in any of the many wonderful campus activities and social functions offered here and eliminate the safety issues associated with alcohol consumption and driving.

**Speaking Passage 1: A conversation between a male student and a female student**

> **Practice Audio: Speaking Passage 1: Conversation**
> Visit mometrix.com/academy and enter Code: 161619

**Question:** *The male student expresses his opinion of the University's new parking permit policy. State and explain his opinion and compare it with the University's Public Service Department's opinion.*

Preparation Time: 30 seconds
Response Time: 60 seconds

**4. Read the passage from a psychology textbook and the lecture that follows it. Then, answer the question. (Reading time in an actual test would be 45-50 seconds.)**

*THEORY OF MIND*

Theory of mind posits that humans have their own minds that they are aware of through intuition and introspection. We cannot directly see our own minds, and for this reason, the term "theory" is ascribed to the phenomenon, since the "mind" is somewhat intangible. Therefore, the word "law" cannot be applied because observations are not made with a concrete, reproducible model or specimen that can be proven after rigorous experimentation and application of the scientific method. Theory of mind allows an individual to understand via analogy, reciprocity, social interaction, and recognizing similar experiences from their own life that another person must also have a mind with desires and perspectives. When an individual demonstrates an effective theory of mind, he or she is able to understand the emotions, thoughts, motivations, and mental state of another and use this awareness to "read" and evaluate this information in such a way as to explain and predict the other person's behavior. Research indicates that humans develop the ability to understand the mental states and emotions of others through the course of normal, healthy social and cognitive development, by interacting, observing, and imitating others and by paying attention to other people and their interactions and behavior.

**Speaking Passage 2: A lecture by a male professor**

> **Practice Audio: <u>Speaking Passage 2: Lecture</u>**
> Visit mometrix.com/academy and enter Code: 414825

**Question:** Explain theory of mind and how the professor's example illustrates the concept.

    Preparation Time: 30 seconds
    Response Time: 60 seconds

**5. Read along below as you listen to the conversation between two students and then answer the question that follows.**

**Practice Audio: Speaking Passage 3: Conversation**
Visit mometrix.com/academy and enter Code: 861389

Male student: Hey Kate! Long time no see! Can you believe the semester is almost over?

Female student: Ugh, don't remind me. I'm stressed about my summer break plans.

Male student: Oh. I can't wait for the break! I'll get to sleep in and eat all of my mom's home cooked meals. Why are you stressed?

Female student: Well, my mom's best friend hired me to work in her real estate office this summer, mostly doing administrative work. The money is really good and she's going to train me to become a certified agent as well. But, I just found out yesterday that I was accepted into a prestigious internship program at the hospital here near school that I applied to a couple of months ago.

Male student: Oh wow! Congratulations! Is that the internship program associated with the University's medical school?

Female student: Yes, it is. It looks like a really great opportunity to learn about medicine because you get to do rotations with physicians in several departments around the hospital and I want to be a doctor, but it is unpaid and I really need money for tuition and bills next year. Plus, I already committed to my mom's friend. She's expecting my help in the office full-time back home.

Male student: Ah, yeah that's important too. Are you interested in real estate? If you got certified as an agent, would you enjoy that work?

Female student: I guess. It certainly isn't as appealing of a career to me but, in the short term at least, I would be setting myself up better financially. If I do the internship, I also have to pay for room and board over the summer here at the University and a $1000 fee for an insurance policy to cover me working with patients in the hospital. With the real estate job, I'd live at home with my parents and avoid all of those expenses, plus I'd get paid.

Male student: Geez. That is tough. Now I understand why you're stressed about summer break. At least you have two good options. When do you have to decide?

Female student: I only have until Friday to turn in my paperwork and pay my deposit for the internship or I'll lose my spot. I guess I better go make a pro/con list and think about it!

Male student: Good luck, Kate!

**Question: Briefly summarize Kate's problem and the two options. Then, state which solution you would recommend. Be sure to explain the reasons for your recommendation.**

Preparation Time: 20 seconds
Response Time: 60 seconds

**6. Read along below as you listen to part of a lecture in an earth science course and then answer the question that follows.**

## LECTURE TRANSCRIPT

Female Professor: So, we are going to pick up today with our discussion of astronomy and start talking about the moon. Earth's moon is actually the largest satellite relative to its planet's size in our solar system, so essentially, while several other planets have a moon or multiple moons, none of the other moons are as closely related in size to their planet as our moon is to Earth. The prevailing theory is that a collision between a celestial body about the size of Mars and the semi-molten Earth of 4.5 billion years ago ejected rocky debris that was adopted into Earth's orbit. Over time, this material condensed into the moon, which had a smaller core and less density than that of Earth.

Our understanding of the lunar surface mostly comes from information from the Apollo missions that included radiometric rock dating and studies of crater densities. The moon's surface has both dark lowlands, called *maria* because they were thought to resemble the smooth sea, and brighter highlands that are studded with craters. The contrast of these two regions gives the moon its "face" appearance. The maria are formed from basaltic lavas that form smooth plains and cover roughly 16% of the surface of the moon. There are very few large volcanic cones in these areas. Instead, there are frequent eruptions of liquidy basaltic lava. The *terrae* are the light-colored areas and so named because terrae means "lands." These are the lunar highlands, so they are several kilometers higher than the maria and are mainly formed from rocks called *breccias.*

The lunar surface also has several impact craters from different collisions. There are two relatively young craters, named Kepler and Copernicus. Do you remember reading about those notable astronomers in our textbook? Anyway, these, and other moon craters, formed from bombardment by celestial bodies of at least one kilometer in diameter.

One interesting fact is that the moon's rotation, or its axis spin, and revolution around the Earth are equal, so the same side always faces Earth. We will discuss this more in our next class though, when we explore the phases of the moon.

**Question:** Using points and information from the lecture, describe the lunar surface as detailed by the professor.

Preparation Time: 20 seconds
Response Time: 60 seconds

# Writing

## ADDITIONAL INSTRUCTIONS FOR THE TEST

On the TOEFL, you will be given two writing tasks to complete. The first task is the **integrated writing task** in which you will read a short excerpt from a university level text and then listen to a lecture corresponding to the text. You must then write a response to a question asking about the main ideas and how the two sources of information relate. Your response should be between 150 and 225 words, although exceeding this amount is acceptable so long as the question is answered effectively.

The second writing task is the **independent writing task**, which requires you to answer a question based upon your own personal experience. This may be asking if you agree or disagree with a statement and what reasons you have for thinking so. Responses for the independent writing task should be at least 300 words.

*The following reading passage and lecture are used for Writing Task 1. Use the following space or scratch paper to answer the following questions.*

## READING PASSAGE

### *SPEAKING THROUGH SOCIAL MEDIA*

The widespread phenomenon of mass communication through cell phones and the Internet has spurred enormous controversy. Many believe that people have become less able to build bonds with friends and family members. It is impossible to deny that social media is constantly changing the way that people interact with one another. With the advent of new technologies that allow for non-simultaneous and distant interaction, people all over the world are now able to build relationships in a way that was formerly not possible. Some might say that this is a negative trend, but this new development opens up unique and effective connections.

People often feel estranged in their surroundings. There are so many hobbies and interests that people enjoy, that it can be difficult to find someone who shares the same passions. Social media is a huge benefit to these people as they are empowered with opportunity for connection to a widespread community and countless resources. Some may have always wanted to learn more about a topic without having an avenue to jump in. Social media has proven itself to be effective in educating people of all ages on a variety of subjects ranging from rollerblading to string theory.

Moreover, the Internet is especially useful for helping people find a voice. Whereas the First Amendment protects our right to free speech, many people feel that they have lost their ability to be heard. Social media allows us all to find a new way to speak confidently and ensures that every person has the opportunity to be heard.

**Writing Passage 1: A lecture by a male professor**

> **Practice Audio: Writing Passage 1: Lecture**
> Visit mometrix.com/academy and enter Code: 395508

## INTEGRATED WRITING TASK

Prompt: Describe the risks discussed in the lecture and explain how they relate to the purpose of the reading passage.

## INDEPENDENT WRITING TASK

Prompt: Is it more important to have talent or hard work? Explain by connecting your answer to your own personal experience.

# Answers and Explanations

## Reading

### PASSAGE 1 ANSWERS AND EXPLANATIONS

**1. D:** All other sentences in the passage offer some support or explanation. Only the sentence in answer choice D indicates an unsupported opinion on the part of the author.

**2. C:** The author actually says, "Charles's own political troubles extended beyond religion in this case, and he was beheaded in 1649." This would indicate that religion was less involved in this situation than in other situations. There is not enough information to infer that Charles II never married; the passage only notes that he had no legitimate children (in fact, he had more than ten illegitimate children by his mistresses.) And while the chance of a Catholic king frightened many in England, it is reaching beyond logical inference to assume that people were relieved when the royal children died. Finally, the author does not provide enough detail for the reader to assume that James I had *no* Catholic leanings. The author only says that James recognized the importance of committing to the Church of England.

**3. A:** The author notes, "In spite of a strong resemblance to the king, the young James was generally rejected among the English and the Lowland Scots, who referred to him as "the Pretender." This indicates that there *was* a resemblance, and this increases the likelihood that the child was, in fact, that of James and Mary Beatrice. Answer choice B is too much of an opinion statement that does not have enough support in the passage. The passage essentially refutes answer choice C by pointing out that James "the Pretender" was welcomed in the Highlands. And there is little in the passage to suggest that James was unable to raise an army and mount an attack.

**4. B:** The passage is arranged in a chronological sequence, with each king introduced in order of reign.

**5. D:** The passage is largely informative in focus, and the author provides extensive detail about this period in English and Scottish history. There is little in the passage to suggest persuasion, and the tone of the passage has no indication of a desire to entertain. Additionally, the passage is historical, so the author avoids expressing feelings and instead focuses on factual information (with the exception of the one opinion statement).

**6. A:** Paragraph two states that "Scholars in the 21st century are far too hasty in dismissing the role of religion in political disputes," which matches answer choice A.

**7. C:** The author states that the people of the Lowlands and England referred to young James as the Pretender, as he bore strong resemblance to the king, but did not hold true lineage to inherit the throne. Later, he would go to attempt to reclaim what he believed to be his rightful throne.

**8. D:** Paragraph three states that "Charles II died without a legitimate heir, and his brother James ascended to the throne as King James II."

**9. C:** This passage includes information about lineage, but generally seeks to inform and convince the reader that religion had a part in fueling conflict between nations, particularly England and Scotland.

76

**10. A:** As a result of his religious and political affiliations, particularly regarding his marriage to the Catholic Princess Henrietta Maria of France, King Charles I was beheaded. Religious groups at this time were very strict with regulating marriages and divorces and did not condone intermarriage with other religions, and had even more effect when regarding the leadership of a country. This further reinforced the author's purpose of demonstrating how religion played a part in political effects within the history of England.

**11. B:** An orphan makes the most sense in this context and is discernable from the other answer choices. Neither a prince nor a nephew would need to be smuggled in. In addition, an illegitimate child was never referred to in this passage, which leaves orphan as the most fitting choice in this context.

**12. B:** Tone refers to the author's voice, or what kind of appeal he is making to the audience. In this passage, the author is attempting to inform the audience of a series of events in the history of English and Scottish royalty. The author is making an appeal, but makes his appeal with a tone that is informative sounding, as he grounds his argument in facts.

**13. A:** Whereas all of these answers are true, Queen Elizabeth's death is not necessary to the rest of the story. King James did commission a Protestant Bible translation, which could have been a major contributor to the conflict. Prince Charlie's and King Charles II's decisions also directly affected the conflict which this passage circulates around.

**14. D:** Whereas all of these answers are legitimate and came from the story, only one came as a result of this battle. The Battle of Culloden ended the confusion of religion between Scotland and England and they became completely Protestant nations.

## PASSAGE 2 ANSWERS AND EXPLANATIONS

**15. D**: The main argument is stated in paragraph 4: "With the progression and extreme convenience of technology, printed books will soon become a thing of the past."

**16. C**: Paragraph 1 explains how stories have progressed, beginning with oral tradition and past the invention of the printing press. In context with the rest of the essay, this paragraph is important in explaining how stories progress and are provided within society.

**17. A**: In paragraph 1, it is stated that oral tradition was the main medium for storytelling before the invention of the printing press.

**18. B**: It is not a fact that "sliding a finger across the screen or pressing a button to read more on the next page is just as satisfying to the reader." Satisfaction is not something universal that can be proven for every reader. This statement is an opinion.

**19. A**: The author makes the argument in paragraph 5 that devices such as the iPad and Kindle are "therefore better than books because they have multiple uses."

**20. B**: The author's purpose in writing this essay is to persuade the reader about the merits of digital media. Although author uses history as part of the contextualization of his argument, and uses comparative information to help justify his points, this is more persuasive than informative due to his desire to convince the reader of the change from print to electronic books.

**21. D**: The author's purpose is evidently persuasive because of his use of captivating language when referring to digital media but not with print media. In addition, the author makes assertions that most people have already given up on print media and focuses on ways in which digital media is better. Print media is still very widely used, if not more used than digital books. The author uses some facts mixed in with opinions to make a convincing argument. If the author had used only facts and presented an unbiased argument, this passage could have been informative rather than argumentative. This passage was clearly not written for entertainment, as it does not seek to simply tell a story or use overtly descriptive language.

**22. B:** Each of these answer choices have merit, and are possibly true, but the only one given for the reason that books are going out of use is that digital media is more convenient. Books were costly when first made, but the passage gives no evidence of this at the moment. There is also no indication within the text provided that people do not like to read or that people still enjoy listening to stories.

**23. C:** In paragraph three, the author lists waiting for appointments, enduring flight durations, and relaxing before sleep as common uses for reading books. While studying for a test is a very effective use for books, the author does not list this as one of his points anywhere in the story.

**24. B:** The author's purpose in writing this passage is to convince the reader that digital books are better than printed books. He even ends the passage with words such as "move forward" and an encouragement that "it is only a matter of time before we must say goodbye to the printed past and welcome the digital and electronic future." This language associates the past with print and the future with electronic, which indicates an excitement for the change, as opposed to resisting change.

**25. C:** Although this story begins by talking about storytelling, it centers more on the media format than on storytelling itself. It also acts more as a persuasive essay and not fully historical or informative. "The Digital Future of Reading" is more fitting than "A History of Print Media."

**26. D:** The author gives a list of large screens, the ability to have several books saved on file, and the ability to recharge a device as reasons that digital media are as good as or better than printed media.

**27. C:** The passage is primarily organized in a chronological sequence to demonstrate progress into the future. At times the author does use comparisons, but looking at each paragraph, the author begins with the early forms of storytelling, continuing into print media, and finally into the modern electronic reading devices. The chronological sequencing contributes to his argument that electronic books are the way of the future.

**28. A:** The author uses a straw man argument to compare why people choose books versus digital reading devices. In paragraph five, the author gives the position that some people prefer printed books by saying that "reading is not complete without turning a page."

**Passage 3 Answers and Explanations**

**29. D:** The main purpose of this passage is to convince the reader that school attendance should not be mandatory because it keeps students who want to learn from actually learning. The author does not go into the details of any attendance policies and only uses the decline in standardized test scores in America as an introduction to his actual topic. Whereas the other answers have pieces of information included in the passage, answer D is the only answer that sums up the main purpose of this passage.

**30. B:** The word *compulsory* is mentioned a few times throughout the passage and is used to mean required or mandatory. This is well indicated by the topic of attendance and using phrases such as "allow only those who are committed to attend." *Frequent* is the only other viable option, but can be disqualified by the context.

**31. C:** The main ideas of this passage indicate a hope for change and even a proposition for doing away with the current policies. He poses himself as having a strong understanding of how the current policies work and advocates against them.

**32. A:** The author begins the passage by stating that standardized test scores are in decline and says that these test scores indicate that the education system is ineffective. The author proceeds to suggest changing laws to improve the system. Answer choices B and C refer to points that the author made throughout, but do not follow the whole of what this passage hopes to accomplish.

**33. A:** The context indicates that these laws are costly as a result of their applications, but do not fully support *expensive* as a viable answer. A better choice would be *outdated*. This particular context indicates that the laws are not functioning but are lingering. The word *vanishing* contradicts the author's intent for using this word.

**34. C:** This passage alludes to the fact that private schools have different regulations than public schools and are more easily able to fail or expel students. Whereas some of the other answer choices are potentially true, the only one that is indicated by paragraph two is answer C.

**35. B:** Each of the answers listed are given in paragraph three in the author's main list of benefits for a change of policy with exception to a decrease in the costs of transporting students.

**36. D:** For this context, the only meaning that could clearly apply is slightly or barely, as the author suggests that students are barely taught in schools with the conditions of the present education system.

**37. D:** Answer D is the best choice because it restates the author's position on the main issue and his plan to resolve the issue.

**38. C:** Answers A, B, and D were not indicated at all by the passage, although they may be true. Answer C was suggested in paragraph 1 – that the students who do not want to come to school are so antagonistic to learning that neither they nor the students who do want to come to school are able to learn effectively. The passage does not suggest any details as to how they might harm or distract other students.

**39. A:** The author uses the word *birthright* in a metaphorical sense to insinuate that all Americans should have the opportunity to receive a good education and that others should not be able to infringe on that right. Birthrights typically refer to familial property inheritances and not necessarily constitutionally or nationally given rights. Answers C and D are not insinuated at all with the passage.

**40. C:** Paragraph three uses the word *recalcitrant* in a negative application describing students that need to be policed. None of the other options describe students that need to be policed, even though they all carry a negative connotation.

**41. B:** The title "So That Nobody Has To Go To School If They Don't Want To" is a more lighthearted sounding title than the serious excerpt that it describes. This could be mocking either those who do not want to attend school or the laws that require all children to go to school. Perhaps the author wrote the title in a lighthearted manner to attract readers rather than seeming overly harsh. Satire often makes use of over- or under-exaggeration, striking a humorous appeal to criticize a serious subject.

**42. B:** Whereas answer A may be a positive byproduct of changing these laws, an increase in grades was not mentioned as a result of changing the law. The author does, however, mention in his third point that grades would begin to show what they are supposed to, likely because teachers would start taking grading more seriously rather than just passing students along whether they are prepared or not. Similarly, answers C and D are not included in the discussion, which leaves B as the proper answer.

# Listening

**1. A:** At the beginning of the conversation, listeners should recall that the female student, Claudia, informs the male student, Miguel, that she is stressed about a big project in her philosophy class. She says, "I love the material we are learning but I'm frustrated by a big assignment that's due next week." She later reveals to Miguel that it's a midterm group project. Miguel was the one who had the bridge project for engineering, so Choice *B* is incorrect. There is no mention of the fact that she is struggling to understand the philosophies; in fact, she says she's enjoying the material, so Choice *C* is wrong. She has not yet received the grade for the midterm because the project is due on Monday, so Choice *D* is incorrect.

**2. A, C:** Claudia says that they must write a 10-page paper and give a 20-minute presentation on notable philosophers.

**3. D:** Commiserating means to sympathize or feel pity for someone else. Miguel has been in a similar situation before – when he had to work on the bridge project with his engineering group but had to do most of the work himself – so he is able to relate to Claudia's situation and feels badly for her. He also says: "I don't envy the situation you're in." This means that he is glad he is not in her situation, because he knows it is not a good one to be in.

**4. B, C:** Claudia says that she feels the people in her group are not taking the project seriously. She tells Miguel: "It's due on Monday and two of the people have yet to start their sections and the other student's piece was terrible." Choice *A* is incorrect because there is no mention that anyone in the group doesn't enjoy the material, just that one did not cover the assigned requirements in his section. Choice *D* is incorrect because there is no mention that anyone in the group doesn't think the project will impact their grade. In contrast, it is mentioned that the project is worth 40% of one's overall course grade.

**5. C:** When Miguel says that he "had to carry the weight of the whole group since no one held up their end" he means that he had to take on the bulk of the work. He adds, "It was so much work to do by myself." This is a figure of speech and not to be taken literally; it does not relate to the bridge supporting a certain weight before collapsing as indicated in Choices *A* and *D*. It also does not indicate that he managed the others' work, just that he did most of the work himself.

**6. A:** Claudia says, "Before this, I always loved group projects, but now, my opinion has shifted" to convey that she used to love group projects but now that has changed (shifted) due to the current negative experience with her group, so she no longer likes them. Choice *B* essentially reverses her shift. Choices *C* and *D* may be attractive answers because they relate to philosophy but her statement does not actually relate to the course material but rather, to the assignment, so they are also incorrect.

**7. B:** The main topic of the lecture is the varied ways in which Sensory Processing Disorder impacts students. Listeners hear about the range of symptoms of the disorder, how these symptoms play out in the classroom, and learn that there are various classroom accommodations that may provide assistance to a student with the disorder. Choice *A* is incorrect because it is never mentioned that Sensory Processing Disorder is a learning disability but rather a developmental disorder and regardless, the focus of the lecture is on the specific issue of Sensory Processing Disorder, not learning disabilities at large. Cures for the disorder are not mentioned, so Choice *C* is wrong, and while the students listening to the lecture are in an education class and likely want to become teachers, the lecture is not about how to teach them, so Choice *D* is wrong.

**8. B:** The professor says that "integration issues can manifest in a variety of ways because there are several senses and the reliance on them overlaps in most situations...it's very rare that you only see something, but there is no auditory input, or that you'd taste something without also having some degree of smell input. With integration issues, sometimes it is these combinations that create issues with interpreting the signal." Essentially, sensory input among the five senses is often concurrent and interrelated, which can make the simultaneous processing and combining of these stimuli challenging for the brain of someone with SPD. The professor adds that "the impact of SPD on an individual can be far-reaching because of the number of senses and the way in which they interact in an integrated way normally, to help us make sense of our environment and our body within the environment." Choice *A* is incorrect because, although true, it does not answer the question posed. Choice *C* is incorrect because an individual with SPD may be both a sensory seeker and sensory-defensive, but this is not always (and in fact, not often) the case. While Choice *D* (that SPD used to be called Sensory Integration Disorder) is true and has to do with integration, it does not answer *why* someone with SPD has integration issues.

**9. A:** The professor explains the variety of ways that SPD may present in a person because the students he is speaking to want to become teachers and they will likely encounter students with SPD. The end of the lecture also makes it clear that there are classroom accommodations and ways that teachers can modify their instruction to help students with Sensory Processing Disorder, which again will be helpful to discuss because many of the students listening to the lecture want to become teachers. This is evidenced by the fact that the professor says, "Today, we are continuing our discussion of different developmental and neurological disorders that your future students may have."

**10. A:** *Comorbidities* are two or more coexisting medical or health conditions. The only answer choice that provides two conditions is Choice *A*, SPD and autism. In fact, these are often concurrent disorders. As the professor explains, "Sensory Processing Disorder is often accompanied by other learning disorders or behavioral and developmental issues, such as autism, ADHD, and anxiety disorders. If students have concurrent disorders, or what we refer to as comorbidities, these should be considered in conjunction when determining classroom accommodations and overall treatment." Touch and hearing (Choice *B*) are both senses, but are not considered comorbid conditions because they are not abnormalities.

**11. D:** The professor does not cover the specific OT techniques and classroom accommodations because he says that the textbook does a good job covering that material. The listening passage ends with his comment: "Your textbook does a good job covering suggested classroom accommodations for all sorts of SPD-related challenges, so let's review particular OT strategies and classroom modifications next class after your reading assignment." While the time remaining in class may be running out (Choice *C*), this is not the reason he cites, so test takers should not infer this information, but should instead use the evidence directly stated in the passage.

**12. A:** The professor spends a great deal of time discussing the challenges of understanding and recognizing SPD because of its varied presentation, particularly in regards to the two markedly different subtypes: those who are sensory seekers and those who are sensory defensive.

**13. C:** Although all of the provided answer choices are things that someone with SPD (or even someone without SPD) might struggle with, reading a book in a noisy classroom is the most logical choice given the information in the lecture. The professor mentions that many people with SPD are particularly bothered by noises and reading is an activity that tends to require a quiet environment anyway. Stopping to smell the roses (Choice *A*) is really just a figure of speech meaning that someone is in a rush and not enjoying the moment. Besides the fact that this choice is not often used in its literal sense, even if it were in this case, someone with SPD would likely not enjoy the smell of roses because the fragrance could bombard their olfactory (smell) sense. Choice *B*, chewing food adequately, is not discussed as an issue and Choice *D*, differentiating colors is also not mentioned as an issue; that sounds more like colorblindness.

**14. A:** This lecture is mainly focused on the differences between Theravada and Mahayana Buddhism, which are two sects of Buddhism that divided from one another when there were disagreements about the fundamental concepts of the religion. While the fact that Chinese Buddhism took off in different directions than its Indian Buddhism's roots is mentioned (Choice *B*), this is not the main topic of the lecture. Choice *C* is incorrect because meditation is mentioned, but not the different ways meditation is used. The importance of a religion appealing to the masses was an ideal in Mahayana Buddhism, this was not the overall guiding focus of the lecture, making Choice *D* incorrect.

**15. B:** The lecture focuses significant attention to the fact that Theravada and Mahayana Buddhism differed from one another in the sense that for the most part Theravada was only accessible to the upper classes, due to the emphasis it placed on meditation (which was not possible for the working classes because they lacked sufficient leisure time), while Mahayana was designed to be accessible to the masses by removing this requirement. Choice *A* is wrong because the lecture is focusing on both of these sects of Buddhism as practiced in Chinese history. Choice *C* is wrong since Mahayana Buddhism split from Theravada in response to factors of Theravada Buddhism that some people disagreed with. Therefore, Theravada Buddhism preceded Mahayana Buddhism. Choice *D* is wrong because it reverses the information provided in the lecture about the focus on meditation.

**16. C:** "We've only just started to scratch the surface here" means that the topic is just beginning to be explored. The professor says, "I know we've only just started to scratch the surface here and there is a lot of layers we'll get to uncover about these sects in the coming days, but in an effort to not overwhelm you, let's end here a bit early and pick up next class." The class will have a lot more "layers to uncover," meaning there is a lot more to learn and discover in future classes. This phrase is a figure of speech and not to be taken with a literal meaning, so Choice *D* is wrong.

**17. B:** The professor implies that when Buddhism came to China from India, it underwent many changes because China had its own culture and language. This new context allowed the religion to be particularly "malleable" or flexible and easily changeable (so Choice *C* is incorrect). She further explains, "When followers of the same religion begin to disagree on fundamental issues, the religion inevitably splits to form two new interpretations of the original. Today, we are going to talk about the first of these splits, which resulted in the formation of the Mahayana and Theravada branches of Buddhism." Choice *A* is wrong, because it is quite clear that the religion did not have a simple, linear path of evolution, which is why the whole lecture revolves around one of the many splits that occurred over time. To this end, a consensus vote did not dictate the direction of the religion (Choice *D*). Splits occurred when people disagreed about fundamental concepts. A majority vote was not needed to approve a change or new sect.

**18. A, B:** The Four Noble Truths ("all known existence is suffering, suffering is caused by desire, one must eliminate desire to eliminate suffering, and one must follow the eightfold path in order to eliminate desire") and the eightfold path ("maintaining the Right View, Right Intention, Right Speech, Right Action, Right Livelihood, Right Effort, Right Mindfulness, and uh...Right Concentration") are central tenants in Theravada Buddhism. Choice *C* is incorrect because Theravada focused a great deal on meditation, so a great deal of one's time was to be dedicated to deep mediation, which made it less accessible to "the masses" because meditation takes a lot of time and working class Chinese people had to work and could not dedicate so much time to unpaid meditation. While Mahayanas considered Theravada to be the "Lesser Vehicle" (Hinayana), this is not a component of the sect and therefore, Choice *D* is incorrect.

**19. D:** As mentioned, Theravada was inaccessible to the masses because of the significant time requirement to meditate. The professor says, "This made Theravada Buddhism an esoteric religion because the people of the lower and middle classes were unable to devote so much time to meditation." Something that is *esoteric* is reserved for a select group of people or only understood by a certain group, so it is obscure. Choice *C* is the opposite so it is incorrect. Things that are esoteric can be confusing (Choice *A*) to those who do not possess the necessary knowledge or skill to understand them, but confusing and irrational is not really what esoteric means. Again, Choice *B* may look like a possibly correct answer since, in this case, Theravada was "hard to afford" for the lower classes, but this is more of a coincidence in this case and does not directly correlate with the definition.

**20. D:** This student's measurements are precise but not accurate. Test takers should recall the response from the female student that explains this concept well: "Accuracy refers to the closeness of a measured value to a standard or known value. For example, hmmm... if you obtain a weight measurement of 3.8 kg for a given substance, but the actual weight is 10 kg, then your measurement is not accurate. Precision, on the other hand, refers to like the closeness of two or more measurements of the same item to each other. Using the same example, if you weigh a given object five times, and get 3.6 kg each time, then your measurement is very precise." The geology student's rock samples are very much like her example of precise but inaccurate measurements.

**21. A:** A person's gender is measured on the nominal scale, which is also called the categorical scale because it simply assigns values to categories without any rank or order attached to the categories. The professor also mentions this specific example at the end of the lecture when he says: "For instance, we know gender is nominal. It's generally easy to identify someone as male or female so you are less likely to make a mistake." Even test takers who are uncomfortable with statistics can recall the example from the lecture.

**22. C:** "You hit the nail on the head" is a phrase that means, "you are right on!" or "You are correct!" Coincidentally, it can be related to the lecture material: it's like hitting the bull's-eye, being both accurate and precise.

**23. B:** This lecture discussion took place in a statistics course and would be most applicable to students when conducting experiments or research. Listeners should recall that the professor says, "We've been looking at the hierarchy of the four scales of measurement we use in research, which will be important for you to consider as you design your own experiments and evaluate research."

**24. D:** The lecture discussion is structured to address the four levels of measurement scales in order of increasing specificity. This is essentially the key takeaway of the lecture. Choice *A*, order of importance, may be an attractive answer, but the professor never says one is more important than the other, just that they have different levels of specificity, accuracy, and precision. Different things have to be measured on certain scales but they aren't necessarily more important than one another. There is no cause and effect (Choice *B*) or chronology (Choice *C*) pertinent to the lecture's organization.

**25. A:** The ability to paraphrase is important and will be assessed on the TOEFL. Something that is well-paraphrased should be somewhat more concise and simple than the original sentence, while still maintaining its accuracy and important points. The provided sentence was: "Interval scales are essentially an intermediary between the lack of specificity of nominal and ordinal but a little less defined than ratio with no absolute zero, so I think we cannot be quite as precise as ratio but more than the lower levels of measurement." Of the options provided, Choice *A* was the best way to paraphrase this: Interval scale measurements are more specific and thus more precise than nominal and ordinal scales but less precise than ratio scales because they lack an absolute zero. Choices *B* and *D* are wrong because they inaccurately report the points from the initial sentence. Choice *C* may look like a sound choice, but it qualifies interval scales as being *better* and the initial sentence never said one was better than another, just more specific. This sentence also omits important information from the parent sentence.

**26. C:** The student is having trouble understanding the chemistry material, particularly balancing equations and different types of bonds. This is evident in the first several exchanges between Connor and his professor. Choice *A* is incorrect because he needs a chemistry tutor but does not want to become one. Choice *B* is wrong because he says he can make it to office hours and Choice *D* is true, in that Connor does not know where the Student Resource Center is, but this is not the main problem he was having. Instead, it is a secondary question that arises during the conversation about his difficulty with the chemistry material.

**27. A, B, D:** The professor asks Connor if he has reviewed the material in his textbook. He confirms that he has, although it was unhelpful (perhaps he needs a Mometrix study guide!). Even though the textbook was confusing and didn't assist Connor's comprehension, it still is a viable resource that the professor cites. She also says, "We have a lot of alternative *resources* that can help you. I'd like you to start coming to my *office hours* twice a week after your trigonometry class. Additionally, I think he would benefit from going to the *Student Resource Center*." There is no mention of receiving assistance on his exam (Choice *C*). The Student Resource Center is located in the library near the reference materials, but studying these materials themselves is not cited by the professor, so Choice *D* is incorrect.

**28. A:** Test takers should recall that in reference to coming to office hours, Connor says: "I can come on Tuesdays and Thursdays after my trigonometry class." Later in the conversation, the professor confirms by saying, "I'd like you to start coming to my office hours twice a week after your trigonometry class."

**29. A, B:** The most helpful part of the conversation that contained this information was the professor's explanation of what the Student Resource Center is. She says: "It's a room in the library on the second floor with all of the reference materials. The University has a bunch of paid tutors who work with students in a variety of subjects. It's free for all undergraduate students because it is included in your tuition bill, and graduate students just pay a nominal fee." She follows up by adding, "There are several great tutors to cover all of the sciences, including chemistry. I will fill out a referral form for you." From this information, test takers can determine that the Student Resource Center is on the second floor of the library (Choice *A*) and that you need a referral (Choice *B*). Choice *C* is wrong because there are a variety of tutors in all subjects, not just science, and Choice *D* is incorrect because the services are free for undergraduates but graduates must pay a small fee.

**30. B:** "Availability wasn't the limiting factor; I think it was my pride" is best equated in the sentence: "I honestly wasn't too busy; I think I just didn't want to admit that I needed help." The limiting factor refers to what got in the way of accomplishing or doing something. Connor says availability (or time) was not the limiting factor, so he is not "too busy." When "pride gets in the way" it means that a person does not want to show or reveal that he or she doesn't understand something because that would be embarrassing and would negatively impact his or her self-esteem.

**31. D:** Connor mentioned that he did refer to his textbook to try and review the material but that he found the writing dense (hard to understand and read) and the examples seemed confusing.

**32. B:** The main topic of the lecture is the complicated psychology of the character Lady Macbeth in Shakespeare's *Macbeth*. Choices *A* and *C* are mentioned, but they are details of the lecture rather than the central point. Choice *D* is not explicitly mentioned in the lecture, so it is also incorrect.

**33. D:** When the professor says, "I can see I'm losing some of you..." she is implying that her students are losing focus (she is losing their attention on her lecture). In this case, she believes it is because they are worried about their exam grades. She says: "I can see I'm losing some of you because I bet many of you have your minds on last week's midterm, so let's end our discussion here today and go over your test..." The other answer choices do not correctly translate this figure of speech.

**34. B:** Questions that are posed during arguments but are not given a pause to receive actual answers are called rhetorical questions. This is a device used to help strengthen one's argument by engaging listeners and tasking them to examine their own thoughts as they consider the argument. The professor employs this device when she asks, "Do you guys see how the key to Lady Macbeth's strategy for gaining influence over her husband is to somewhat switch the gender roles within her marriage?"

**35. B:** The professor argues that the strength of Shakespeare's plays and a quality that makes him a successful playwright in history is the fact that his works consider the complexities of human nature through character development. At the beginning of the lecture, she says: "As we've been discussing, one element of Shakespeare's writing that sets him apart from his predecessors, and arguably made him a great playwright, was his ability to create characters with intricate and interesting psychologies... These complexities um...evoke his audience's sympathies, and subsequently heightens their interest in the play." Choice *A* is a true statement, but it doesn't answer *why* he is considered a great playwright. While some of his characters are deviant (such as Lady Macbeth), Shakespeare's plays don't necessarily *persuade* audience members to be deviant, so Choice *C* is incorrect. Choice *D* is not really mentioned in the lecture; while specific characters and kings are named, this is not emphasized as Shakespeare's lasting literary impact.

**36. C:** As mentioned, the professor argues that Shakespeare's characters were complex and Lady Macbeth is no exception. Therefore, she would likely think that Lady Macbeth is character who is realistic in her psychological complexities. She mentions that one of Shakespeare's strengths as a playwright was the development of characters with "intricate and interesting psychologies." As she explains: "Many of Shakespeare's main characters are written in general compliance with 'good' and 'evil' archetypes, but just like generally 'good' and 'evil' people in real life, the motives of his characters are complex."

# Speaking

1. Ten years feels like a long time from now so I'm not entirely sure what I will be doing and what my life will look like at that point. Right now, I am studying business at my university and I'm also minoring in marketing. When I graduate in two years, I would like to get my MBA in business. If this plan works out, in 10 years I see myself owning my own small financial consulting company with a handful of employees under my supervision. I would like to move back to the West Coast, around the Los Angeles area, to be closer to my family. My parents should be retired at that point, and I'd like to be closer to them in case they need help as they age. Perhaps I will also be starting a family of my own, after getting married and buying a home with my future wife. I come from a large family and have many brothers and sisters, which was so much fun growing up, so I would also like to have several children. I also hope that my consulting firm is thriving so I can pay off my student loan debt and buy a nice house near Malibu. My siblings and I grew up surfing, so it would be fun to eventually get back into that.

2. I prefer when classes meet at least two to three times per week rather than just one long session. I find that it's hard for me to sit through a class that is more than an hour or so, and some courses offered by the university that only meet once a week are nearly four hours! I really struggle to maintain focus much longer than an hour and my hand gets tired from taking notes. Even if the professor gives a break, it never fully rejuvenates me. The other issue I have with classes that only meet once a week is that it is hard to remember to keep up with the work. After you get through the marathon-session, you're so relieved to be done that it's easy to just dump the books in your room and before you know it, the week has rolled by and you haven't started on the work. When they meet every other day or so, you're forced to stay on top of the material better. Lastly, if you get sick and have to miss a class, if that's the one day the class meets, it's a big hassle to make up the work, and for that reason, some professors don't even allow absences without significantly penalizing your grade.

3. The male student, Adam, is unhappy about the University's decision that freshmen and sophomore students will no longer be allowed to purchase campus parking permits. He has a car and enjoys getting off campus to see movies or shoot pool with his friends and thinks that as long as a student can afford it, they should be able to buy the permit. On the other hand, the University Public Safety and Parking Services department thinks that returning to the junior and senior only policy is in the best interest of the students because there aren't enough spaces for all interested students, so the permit fees are really expensive, which isn't fair for students with financial restrictions. It also will allow all upperclassmen who want to have their cars on campus to do so instead of relying on the current lottery system. Lastly, the University administrators think that this decision will encourage underclassmen to try free campus activities sponsored by the University and prevent drunk driving.

4. Theory of mind is an idea closely related to empathy, that describes the awareness and appreciation that humans can have that other humans also have a mind with unique thoughts, desires, and intentions. When a person develops a healthy and effective theory of mind, that person can not only recognize another person's thoughts and feelings, but also use that information and their own experiences to anticipate and rationalize the other person's intentions and behaviors. The professor's example of the autistic female he worked with in graduate school demonstrates what happens when someone lacks a well-developed theory of mind. This young woman had difficulty in her social interactions because she often misunderstood the feelings, knowledge, and interests of her peers. For example, it was challenging for her to grasp the concept that other people may have less experience and less interest in computer games. Lacking an effective theory of mind

made it hard for her to imagine the differing experiences, opinions, and feelings of others around her.

5. Kate needs to decide how she is going to spend her summer break. She can either work in her mom's friend's real estate office making good money and honoring her previous commitment to work there or she can participate in an unpaid school internship at the medical school that she was just accepted into. It's a difficult decision because she is more interested in becoming a doctor than becoming a real estate agent, but she has already committed to her mom's friend and she'd like to honor that commitment. Additionally, the finances of the two decisions are vastly different. She will have no expenses if she takes the real estate job because she will live at home. She also will be well-paid for her work. In contrast, the internship costs $1000 and she will incur expenses for housing and food on campus. I would still recommend that she participates in the medical internship. She can explain to her mom's friend about the significance of this opportunity, attributable to both the fact that it's a prestigious program and that she really wants to go to medical school eventually to become a doctor in her own right. This internship may help facilitate that path. I imagine that her mom's friend will want what's best for her and as long as Kate notifies her soon, the woman can probably hire another summer employee. I think it's more important that Kate follow her passion and do something that will prepare her for a career she will enjoy. She can research loans or scholarships for the internship to help cover costs. Additionally, pursuing a career in medicine should eventually be lucrative so it is also a practical choice.

6. This lecture described Earth's moon and focused on describing the lunar surface, which is the topography of the moon. The professor explains that our knowledge of the surface features mostly comes from the data obtained from the Apollo missions, where the astronauts conducted radiometric rock dating and studies of the densities of different craters. She explains that the moon's face appearance is created by the fact that the surface has lowlands that are dark, called maria, and highlands, called terrae, which are brighter and contain the various craters. The maria and terrae are formed by different processes. The maria are smooth plains formed from liquidy basaltic lava flows, rather than violent eruptions from big volcano cones. The terrae are formed from rocks and lie several kilometers above the lowlands. Lastly, the lunar surface also has several impact craters from different collisions from large and small celestial bodies.

# Writing

## INTEGRATED WRITING TASK SAMPLE ANSWER

Prompt: Describe the risks discussed in the lecture and explain how they relate to the purpose of the reading passage.

The lecture discouraged social networking by discussing how social networking has many risks. First, the lecture talks about how the Internet can be used to steal or to bully people, including both adults and children. The second point is the main point, however, which explains statistics about how people trusted fewer people with important matters. This suggests that relying on the Internet is causing people to be isolated and not spend as much time with people. Overall, the lecture suggests that social networking has too many risks and is leading our culture in a bad direction.

The lecture and reading passage have opposing views about the use of social media. The reading passage listed several positive qualities of using social media, such as how it helps people learn about hobbies and meet people with the same interests. It also encouraged social media use to help people find a voice. It says that people sometimes have a hard time finding people around them with the same interests, but that through social media, they can find friends.

The lecture and the reading passage both talk about the good and bad effects of social media. The two passages agree on almost nothing except to be careful with new technology. Whereas the lecture focuses mainly on risks, the reading passage focuses on convincing the reader that the rewards outweigh the risks.

### Answer Explanation

This answer is a good response because it addresses the question directly. The first paragraph describes the lecture as requested and the second paragraph describes the reading passage so that the final paragraph can make good comparisons. The main purpose of each passage is given and it is explained how the two selections disagree completely on the outcome of the topic. Grammar is also a consideration in the grading of this selection. When responding, make sure you are using good grammar while also making sure to answer exactly what the question is asking.

## INDEPENDENT WRITING TASK

Prompt: Is it more important to have talent or hard work? Explain by connecting your answer to your own personal experience.

In my experience, having talent only gets you so far. When I first began running long distance, I was slower and became out of breath far before other runners my age did. It took me a surprisingly short amount of time to learn to breathe better and grow stronger in my running. In what seemed like no time at all, I was starting to keep up with my friends. The hard work was beginning to pay off.

Running was not something that I was very comfortable with. I had the wrong body type, and had never done running before. In all honesty, it probably took me more work than it would have for someone who was a natural-born, talented runner. Even though it was so difficult to start out, my determination allowed me to work hard and close the gap between me and those who were more talented. Talent had nothing to do with my success as a runner.

The natural runners that I would learn from had hardly any advice to give me because it came to them almost effortlessly. They would not eat well and would not practice working on their form,

89

which led to them making smaller gains than I would. It seemed like all of my time practicing made me want to rest better and make sure my muscles were healed properly before practicing again. In short, running was so hard for me that I had to take it seriously to do well. That seriousness is what made me a better runner in the long run than the natural athletes.

Since my start at running, I have run several races and even won a few. I may still not be the fastest person alive, but my hard work and determination have paid off in ways that I cannot describe. Hard work has carried me through life far more than talent could ever have done.

## Answer Explanation

This response is good because it answers the question directly from the start, which helps guide the reader in interpreting the personal experience given. The personal experience follows by telling a story of how hard work paid off more than having talent would have. Many responses may only tell how hard work is helpful, but neglect to tell how talent was not as helpful. Answers should try to cover both sides of the argument to be well rounded. There is no incorrect answer for a question like this, so long as the answer is clear and is supported well enough. After laying out all of the evidence, try to wrap the argument up by restating your answer. As always, answers should have strong grammar and overall good spelling.

# Transcripts of Audio Recordings

## LISTENING PASSAGE 1: CONVERSATION TRANSCRIPT

*Narrator: Listen to the following conversation between two students and then answer the following questions.*

Male student: Hi Claudia, how's your philosophy class?

Female student: Oh, hey Miguel, it's pretty good. I love the material we are learning but I'm frustrated with a big assignment that's due next week.

Male student: Oh no. Why's that?

Female student: Well, it's a group project and we have to write a 10-page paper and prepare a 20-minute presentation about different notable philosophers, but my group doesn't seem to be taking the assignment seriously.

Male student: That sounds stressful. Does it count for a large percentage of your course grade?

Female student: Yes, that's the thing. This is our midterm project so it is worth 40% of our total grade. It's due on Monday and two of the people have yet to start their sections and the other student's piece was terrible.

Male student: Oh...what was wrong with it?

Female student: It really didn't satisfy any of the assignment requirements. His job was to cover Aristotle. Our professor gave us specific criteria to address for each philosopher, like where and when they were born, their primary ideas and interests, and who they influenced and who influenced them. Brian, the guy in my group, just focused on Ancient Greece in general and barely mentioned Aristotle, let alone his philosophical contributions!

Male students: That's awful. You know, that's the reason why I find group projects to be stressful. You never know who is going to be in your group and how motivated they are. Sometimes you end up having to do the nearly the whole project yourself or settle for a poor grade. Last year in my engineering class we had to design a suspension bridge using renewable resources in small groups. I had to carry the weight of the whole group since no one held up their end. It was so much work to do by myself.

Female student: Yeah...not fair. I might have to do that for this project. Before this, I always loved group projects, but now, my opinion has shifted.

Male student: Well Claudia, I wish you luck with the project. I don't envy the situation you're in.

Female student: Thanks for commiserating with me, Miguel. Have a nice afternoon.

## LISTENING PASSAGE 2: LECTURE TRANSCRIPT

*Narrator: Listen to the following part of a lecture on Sensory Processing Disorder from an education class.*

Male professor: Ok everyone. Let's settle down and get started. Today, we are continuing our discussion of different developmental and neurological disorders that your future students may have. We are going to turn our attention to Sensory Processing Disorder, or SPD, which is increasingly entering into the dialogue of educators, as awareness and diagnosis increase. In addition to affecting the five senses (touch, smell, taste, vision, and hearing), SPD can manifest in issues with proprioception, vestibular function, and interoception, which is one's awareness of internal stimuli like hunger. I want to stress that SPD has a variety of presentations and it's likely that any two students in your classrooms with SPD may seem almost more different from one another than the same!

Individuals with SPD can be sensory-defensive or sensory-seeking, although these two are not always um...mutually exclusive. For example, someone may be sensory defensive when it comes to auditory stimuli, in which case, he or she has a very low tolerance for noises and becomes easily overwhelmed with sounds. That same person may be a sensory seeker with movement, and constantly desire movement and pressure. It is much more common that a person is either a seeker or defensive though. In general, sensory seekers have a very high threshold for the sensory stimuli; they need a lot of it for their brain to process the signal and feel satisfied. Those who are sensory defensive, have very low thresholds, so they cannot tolerate much input before becoming overwhelmed or even physically ill.

In addition to issues with thresholds for sensory stimuli, there are often issues integrating the sensory information. Actually, the disorder used to be called sensory integration disorder, so some of you may have heard of that terminology instead. Anyway, integration issues can manifest in a variety of ways because there are several senses and the reliance on them overlaps in most situations. For example, it's very rare that you only see something, but there is no auditory input, or that you'd taste something without also having some degree of smell input. With integration issues, sometimes it is these combinations that create issues with interpreting the signal. More often, there is an issue processing a given type of input. For example, someone with SPD may hear an annoying sound but completely lack the ability to point to the direction in which it is coming.

The impact of SPD on an individual can be far-reaching because of the number of senses and the way in which they interact in an integrated way normally, to help us make sense of our environment and our body within the environment. Those with sensory-defensiveness tend to get easily overwhelmed and physically uncomfortable and normal, everyday environments like classrooms, shopping centers, and even the home, because everything is essentially "too much" – too loud, too bright, too chaotic, etc.

Young children who are unable to fully express their feelings are often seen as picky, immature, or out-of-control. In the toddler population, kids with SPD are often tantruming, they may experience late potty training, they can be hard to calm and have difficulty sleeping, and sensory seekers are often found crashing into things, jumping, eating ice, yelling, etc. In the classroom, students with SPD often have issues with handwriting, copying from the board, tolerating noisy lunchrooms, making smooth transitions, and having a good awareness of their body's position in space.

Occupational therapy, which you may have heard referred to as OT, is the most frequently cited specialized service to help students with SPD cope with symptoms and be more comfortable. The therapist can work with the student and also advise the parents and teachers of modifications and techniques to facilitate the student's comfort. The specific OT services that a student may receive vary according to their needs and presentation of the disorder as well as any concomitant challenges.

Actually, that's another important point to emphasize. Sensory Processing Disorder is often accompanied by other learning disorders or behavioral and developmental issues, such as autism, ADHD, and anxiety disorders. If students have concurrent disorders, or what we refer to as comorbidities, these should be considered in conjunction when determining classroom accommodations and overall treatment. Your textbook does a good job covering suggested classroom accommodations for all sorts of SPD-related challenges, so let's review particular OT strategies and classroom modifications next class after your reading assignment.

## LISTENING PASSAGE 3: LECTURE TRANSCRIPT

*Narrator: Listen to part of a lecture from a world religions class and then answer the questions.*

Female Professor: So, recall that we've been looking at how Buddhism in China has evolved in many different directions. Adapting the religion from its Indian origins into a uh...Chinese context had inherent difficulties, due to the differences in culture, language, and epistemologies. This left Buddhism in an especially malleable state in China, which um...provides some explanation as to how so many different forms of Buddhism came to exist. Each branch of Buddhism takes a different approach in the recruitment and education of followers. When followers of the same religion begin to disagree on fundamental issues, the religion inevitably splits to form two new interpretations of the original. Today, we are going to talk about the first of these splits, which resulted in the formation of the Mahayana and Theravada branches of Buddhism.

Theravada Buddhism is based on the "Four Noble Truths": all known existence is suffering, suffering is caused by desire, one must eliminate desire to eliminate suffering, and one must follow the eightfold path in order to eliminate desire. This eightfold path consisted of maintaining the Right View, Right Intention, Right Speech, Right Action, Right Livelihood, Right Effort, Right Mindfulness, and uh...Right Concentration. Theravada Buddhism focused a great deal on the last section of the eightfold path, which was meditation, so a great deal of one's time was to be dedicated to deep mediation. This made Theravada Buddhism an esoteric religion because the people of the lower and middle classes were unable to devote so much time to meditation. Essentially, only the um...highest classes were able to dedicate their lives to this, because they were the only classes with sufficient leisure time.

Mahayana Buddhists believed that the Theravada form was inaccessible to the great majority of people, due to the extreme emphasis on meditation. The Mahayana Buddhists disagreed so much with the Theravada Buddhists that they even referred to Theravada as Hinayana, or "The Lesser Vehicle."

Actually, this is an important distinction and warrants a pause in our discussion just to reiterate. Theravada and Mahayana Buddhism differ to a great extent in the basic ideology of attracting new followers. Theravada essentially makes little effort to include those who are unable to adhere to the requirements of their religion. The Mahayana Buddhists designed their religion to appeal to a great number of people, you know, basically to be more convenient and understandable to the illiterate masses.

I know we've only just started to scratch the surface here and there is a lot of layers we'll get to uncover about these sects in the coming days, but in an effort to not overwhelm you, let's end here a bit early and pick up next class.

## LISTENING PASSAGE 4: LECTURE AND DISCUSSION TRANSCRIPT

*Narrator: Listen to the following portion of a lecture and discussion from a statistics class.*

Male Professor: So, recall that we've been looking at the hierarchy of the four scales of measurement we use in research, which will be important for you to consider as you design your own experiments and evaluate research. As a quick review, we have nominal, ordinal, interval, and ratio. Nominal scales are the lowest level of measurement. We also refer to them as classificatory scales, wherein objects or people are assigned to categories according to some criterion. Ordinal scale measurements require categories to be rank ordered on the basis of an operationally-defined characteristic or property. For example, customer satisfaction ranked 1-5. Interval scales possess the rank order characteristics of an ordinal scale but there are known equal distances between consecutive units of measurement. This allows relative differences in equivalences within a scale to be determined. Ratio scales achieve the greatest measurement specificity. A ratio scale is an interval scale with an absolute zero point that has empirical, rather than an arbitrary, meaning.

Today I want us to consider the relevance and importance of assessing accuracy and precision within each of these scales. Before we do this though, who is willing to remind us about what accuracy and reliability mean? Yes, Janet.

Female student: Well, uh…accuracy refers to the closeness of a measured value to a standard or known value. For example, hmmm… if you obtain a weight measurement of 3.8 kg for a given substance, but the actual weight is 10 kg, then your measurement is not accurate. Precision, on the other hand, refers to like the closeness of two or more measurements of the same item to each other. Using the same example, if you weigh a given object five times, and get 3.6 kg each time, then your measurement is very precise.

Male professor: Very well said, Janet and those examples were perfect. And remember, precision is independent of accuracy. You can be very precise but inaccurate and you can be accurate but imprecise. So now, let's try to layer this thinking onto our different measurement scales and evaluate them through the lens of their potential accuracy and precision. I'll start with nominal scales and then see if anyone wants to take a stab at any of the others. Ok? Because nominal scales are more like categories, it is hard to have much precision. For example, if the categories are various colors, our values could be blue, red, and green. But the categories will have many shades of each color that all have a common general color but many variations of the hue. Sky blue and navy look very different, right? Accuracy would also be challenging. Continuing with our color example, the delineations between the categories are not very specific. There can be shades of blue that also appear green such as teal, so which category would they go in? One investigator could select green while another chooses blue.

So, let's consider ordinal scales. Remember, they are represented by rank orders divided by intervals that are not always consistent or known. Two subjects assigned in the same rank may in fact be of completely different values. The ordinal scale is not sensitive enough to determine the differences between ranks and is only able to indicate a relative position of certain distribution rather than its true value or quantity. Manual muscle test is an ordinal scale test. Assigning a grade to an individual may be very accurate and precise based on the scale. However, this scale is pretty much useless when comparing two or more individuals since the difference between two scores is hard to be defined. Who is willing to stick their neck out and try interval scales?

Male student: Interval scales are essentially an intermediary between the lack of specificity of nominal and ordinal but a little less defined than ratio with no absolute zero, so I think we cannot be quite as precise as ratio but more than the lower levels of measurement. My hunch is that the artificial zero point that these scales possess decrease its accuracy because the zero points are just arbitrarily chosen.

Male professor: You hit the nail on the head, Donovan! Who wants to try ratio?

Female student: Well, I think because there are essentially an infinite number of values along the continuum in the ratio scale, it is easier to be more precise because the difference from one value to the next is very, very small. I'm not sure about accuracy.

Male professor: Great start. You've hit on an important concept. In general, scales of higher forms of measurement are more precise. Accuracy is also more important in scales like interval and ratio that are higher levels of measurement and may have more specificity to their assigned values. In a sense, the target on the bullseye is smaller, so it seems logical that it would be easier to miss it and be inaccurate more frequently than in large sweeping general categories like nominal and ordinal scales. For instance, we know gender is nominal. It's generally easy to identify someone as male or female so you are less likely to make a mistake. Salary is a ratio measurement and since there are essentially an infinite number of salaries, it would be easier to misreport it and have an accuracy error. Perhaps you inadvertently flip the numbers around, or mishear a fifty as sixty.

## LISTENING PASSAGE 5: CONVERSATION TRANSCRIPT

*Narrator: Listen to the following conversation between a student and his professor and then answer the questions.*

Female professor: Hey Connor, thanks for staying after class. I won't keep you long, but I wanted to talk about your grades and progress in my course.

Male student: Yeah, I've been meaning to come to your office hours for some help. I guess I'm struggling to understand the chemistry material.

Female professor: Well, I'm glad you are trying to be pro-active about your studies and yes, you should always feel free to come to my office hours. If those times don't work for you, I am also happy to meet with you at an alternative time.

Male student: Thanks, but they are fine. I can come on Tuesdays and Thursdays after my trigonometry class. Availability wasn't the limiting factor; I think it was my pride.

Female professor: I appreciate your honesty and don't worry, a lot of students are nervous or shy to ask for help. But the good news is, you are here now we can start addressing your challenges. So, on the last exam, you got a 62. You got most of the questions about acids and bases correct, but it looks like you didn't get any of the chemical structure and bonding questions.

Male student: Yeah, balancing chemical equations went completely over my head and I don't understand the differences between ionic, covalent, and hydrogen bonds.

Female professor: Have you tried looking at this material in the course textbook?

Male student: I tried, but I found the writing to be very dense and the examples were confusing.

Female professor: OK. Don't worry. We have a lot of alternative resources that can help you. I'd like you to start coming to my office hours twice a week after your trigonometry class. Additionally, I think he would benefit from going to the Student Resource Center.

Male student: Hmm...what's that?

Female professor: It's a room in the library on the second floor with all of the reference materials. The University has a bunch of paid tutors who work with students in a variety of subjects. It's free for all undergraduate students because it is included in your tuition bill, and graduate students just pay a nominal fee.

Male student: Wow, that sounds great! I had no idea that we had a resource like that on campus. Do they have chemistry tutors?

Female professor: Yes. There are several great tutors to cover all of the sciences, including chemistry. I will fill out a referral form for you. All you need to do is call or stop by the Student Resource Center and set up an appointment. They will ask you for the referral form and your student ID.

Male student: Perfect. Thanks Professor Winter. I'll get right on this.

Female professor: That's great Connor. There is still plenty of time left in the semester to turn your grade around.

## LISTENING PASSAGE 6: LECTURE TRANSCRIPT

*Narrator: Listen to the lecture in a literature class and then answer the questions.*

Female professor: As we've been discussing, one element of Shakespeare's writing that sets him apart from his predecessors, and arguably made him a great playwright, was his ability to create characters with intricate and interesting psychologies. Many of Shakespeare's main characters are written in general compliance with "good" and "evil" archetypes, but just like generally "good" and "evil" people in real life, the motives of his characters are complex. These complexities um…evoke his audiences' sympathies, and subsequently heightens their interest in the play. Shakespeare's most famous characters are those that do not conform absolutely to typical protagonist and antagonist roles. These characters prevent audiences from considering and appreciating the play on strictly superficial levels.

So, now that we've had to chance to finish Macbeth, I think you'll see how Shakespeare's portrayal of Lady Macbeth contains these additional dimensions that make her character realistic and engaging. In public, she recognizes and behaves within her social limitations and expectations as a woman, but violates those boundaries while alone or with her husband. Lady Macbeth shifts between the passive role of a wife, the aggressive attitude of a leader, and the tempting behaviors of I don't know…a seductress, in order to advance her and her husband's social and financial status.

Lady Macbeth reveals her scheming and violent nature within her first few lines of the play. She is completely aware that she and her husband have common goals, but that without her influence, Macbeth himself lacks the primal instinct needed to commit the murder of King Duncan. Macbeth's horrible vision of murder is not his own, his ambition has been purposefully implanted by his wife. Macbeth's is extremely passive, and speaks in a tone much like that of a scared child; he asks his wife if they are going to be suspected of the murders. Essentially, the moment that Macbeth submits to his wife's leadership is the moment that the traditional marital and gender roles are reversed.

Do you guys see how the key to Lady Macbeth's strategy for gaining influence over her husband is to somewhat switch the gender roles within her marriage? Just before Macbeth arrives home, Lady Macbeth pleads "unsex me here." So, essentially, Lady Macbeth seeks to lose her female restrictions in order to gain total control over the situation, or…uh…what she sees as her opportunity to gain power over her husband. Lady Macbeth successfully "unsexes" herself by assuming the male role and aggressively taking matters into her own hands throughout the play. Lady Macbeth adjusts her language and tone to make herself more masculine in these instances, which intimidate Macbeth's actions in turn.

In order to avoid suspicion, Lady Macbeth alters her behavior for the public eye as well. She knows that self-effacement and politeness are necessary behaviors to adopt so that she and her husband are able to climb social and financial ladders. The tone of her speech as she addresses King Duncan is apologetic and submissive. She behaves this way to put the King at ease, and you know, probably to make him more susceptible to her husband's violence. Lady Macbeth plays both of these contrasting roles at the appropriate times in order to move the play in the direction which is most beneficial to her ambitions.

I can see I'm losing some of you because I bet many of you have your minds on last week's midterm, so let's end our discussion here today and go over your test, but next class, I want to pick up with the different styles of language Lady Macbeth uses to gain what she needs from the other characters in the play.

## SPEAKING PASSAGE 1: CONVERSATION TRANSCRIPT

*Narrator: Listen to the following conversation between two students regarding school parking policies.*

Male student: Hey Janice, did you read about the new parking policy starting in the fall?

Female student: No, I don't drive so I must have skimmed over it. What's happening, Adam?

Male student: Well, the University's Public Safety and Parking Services department decided that starting next year, freshman and sophomore students cannot buy a campus parking permit. Only juniors and seniors will be able to have their cars here. I'm so mad! I'm only going to be a sophomore, so I won't get to keep my car on campus anymore.

Female student: Oh wow! Well, you know, it's actually probably a good idea because there are fewer parking spaces now that they put in the baseball field and it's kind of an unfair advantage for students who don't have financial limitations. I heard they are like $500 a year!

Male student: Yeah, I think they are like $550, but if you can afford it, you should be able to buy one. Plus, it's not like I just use my car myself. I take my roommate and buddies from my dorm out to the movies or to play billiards. They always want rides!

Female student: That sounds fun but you know, the Campus Center has movies every night except Monday and there is a big game room on the second floor with pool tables, air hockey, and foosball. It's really fun. Plus, all this stuff is free.

Male student: I didn't know there was a game room but I bet the movies they show are lame. I like watching movies in the theater. It's a really nice break from being stuck on campus all the time.

Female student: I hear you, but the movie selections they play are actually really good and they're always relatively new releases. Oh, and also, there is the free campus shuttle bus that runs to the shopping mall, grocery store, movie theater, and uh, the downtown area. You could always hop on that to go to the movies.

Male student: Yeah, I guess. I've actually never taken that. I just like driving because you can go whenever you want and aren't slave to the bus schedule.

Female student: Well come try it with me and my friends on Friday! We are going to check out a new cafe downtown. They have karaoke!

Male student: Ok. Maybe. Thanks Janice.

## SPEAKING PASSAGE 2: LECTURE TRANSCRIPT

Professor: So, theory of mind is somewhat similar to empathy, though it expands on this concept by taking it a step further. An effective theory of mind arms the person with the ability to understand and even predict another person's reactions, actions, and feelings. This enables someone to have more meaningful, and arguably, more compassionate and empathetic social interactions by allowing people engaging with one another to attribute thoughts, moods, and intentions to others, to predict or explain their actions and desires. As your text pointed out, these skills, along with perspective-taking and empathy, begin to develop in infancy and are strengthened with healthy and stable social engagement and language exposure. However, when a person has cognitive or developmental disorders, he or she may struggle with theory of mind. Although it's not a hard-and-fast rule, individuals with autism spectrum disorder often demonstrate incomplete or ineffective theories of mind and difficulty with empathy. In graduate school, I did my dissertation on autism and empathy. One young woman I worked with lacked a completely developed theory of mind. She often misinterpreted the feelings and intentions of her peers. She frequently thought that other people hated her when they did not indicate that, and she struggled to understand that other people's opinions and experiences could differ from her own. For example, while she loved talking about computer games, she would become agitated and angry when other people did not demonstrate this passion or didn't have the extensive knowledge base regarding computer games that she had.

## WRITING PASSAGE 1: LECTURE TRANSCRIPT

Male Professor: The effects of social networking come with far too many risks. Many consumers are targeted with phishing schemes that steal people's money or even their identity. These risks do not only extend to adults, but also to children, who are targeted for bullying and manipulation. Children can easily pick up deficits from becoming too reliant on social media for communication. People these days already have a lack of social skills from looking at screens each day. This has already made a clear impact on family systems in America.

A new study by sociologists at Duke University and the University of Arizona adds more grist to this mill, noting that Americans in 2004 had smaller networks of people with whom they talk about matters important to them than they did in 1985. In 1985, the average American had three close confidants. In 2004, we averaged only two. The number of Americans who had no one with whom to talk about important matters almost doubled in 2004 to over 25%. Increasingly, most confidants are family: in 2004, 80% of people talked only to family about important matters, and about 9% people depended totally on their spouse.

This decrease in confidants is, in part, a result of the same trend that's leaving fewer people knowing their neighbors or participating in social clubs or public affairs than in the past. We know a lot of people, but we don't know them very well.

Left to our own devices and cultural trends then, we seem to be moving in an unpleasant direction. Communities are formed ad hoc, around specific shared individual interests. This wouldn't be bad, of course, except that those communities seem to exist only within the constraints of those shared interests, and don't develop into close and meaningful relationships. The transient and specific nature of many of our relationships today can keep us socially busy without building the lasting relationships and communities that we want.

# Common English Language Idioms

- **A blessing in disguise** – a situation which at first seems bad, but which turns out to be a good thing.
- "That red light was a blessing in disguise! If I hadn't stopped when I did, I would have been hit by another car."
- **A dime a dozen** – used when referring to something that is very common.
- "The watch I have is really a dime in a dozen. I really want one that is unique!"
- **Beat around the bush** – to avoid talking about the main topic (usually one which is uncomfortable).
- "Stop beating around the bush and just go tell her you like her."
- **Bite the bullet** – to face a problem or situation immediately rather than avoiding it.
- "I want to ask for two weeks off from work but I am afraid to ask my boss. I guess I should just bite the bullet and ask her."
- **Break a leg** – said as a replacement for telling someone good luck.
- "You'll do great at your performance. Break a leg!"
- **Call it a day** – to stop working for the day.
- "I've made a lot of progress and I'm tired. I'm going to call it a day."
- Can't make heads or tails of something – to not be able to understand something.
- "I've read the example in the textbook three times and I still can't make heads or tails of it."
- **Couch potato** – a lazy person.
- "You should stop being such a couch potato and go outside sometime."
- **Cut somebody some slack** – to allow someone to do something without judgment or hindrance.
- "Cut him some slack! He worked all week and needs some time to relax."
- **Cutting corners** – to only do a job partially or to skip steps in the process.
- "If you want to make good grades, you need to do the work thoroughly and not cut corners."
- **Don't count your chickens until (before) they hatch (they've hatched)** – to consider a payment or positive outcome as being yours before in possession.
- "Don't buy something that expensive just because you think you'll be paid next month. You shouldn't count your chickens before they've hatched!"
- **Drag one's feet** – to delay doing something unpleasant.
- "You should really go to the dentist for that toothache as soon as possible. Don't drag your feet!"
- **Egghead** – someone who is very intelligent.
- "He makes straight As in all of his classes without even studying! What an egghead."
- **Elbow grease** – hard work or a high degree of effort (usually manual labor).
- "Most household fixes don't need special tools; just a screwdriver and a little elbow grease will do it."
- **Easy does it** – a caution to be gentle or careful while performing a task.
- "Set it down slowly. I don't want the piano damaged from moving it. Easy does it."
- **Feeling blue** – to be sad.
- "Why are you sitting in the corner?"
- "I'm just feeling a little blue today."
- **Fit as a fiddle** – to be healthy.
- "I was sick for a couple of weeks, but now I'm as fit as a fiddle!"

102

- **Get something out of your system** – to do something so that you will not want or have to do it later.
- "I really was feeling sad, so I cried for a while to get it out of my system."
- **Get your act together** – to recognize that the previous action was not good enough and try to do better.
- "I've been skipping my reading every night and starting a bad habit. I need to get my act together starting today!"
- **Give someone the benefit of the doubt** – to trust someone without having a reason to do so.
- "He wanted to borrow my truck, but I've never seen him drive. Maybe I should give him the benefit of the doubt and let him have it anyway."
- **Go back to the drawing board** – to have a failed first attempt and try to start over.
- "Well, we tried and did not succeed. Time to go back to the drawing board."
- **Hang in there** – to persevere in a difficult or painful situation.
- "Your job has been really hard lately, but you've done well to hang in there!"
- **Hit the sack** – to go to bed (usually early).
- "I worked so hard today and am exhausted. I think I'll go ahead and hit the sack."
- **In over one's head** – to be in a situation that is too difficult to handle.
- "I'm in a calculus class and don't understand anything. I think I'm in over my head."
- **It takes two to tango** – to state that it is more than one person's responsibility or fault (usually said in a negative way).
- "She and I always fight about our relationship, but it's not all her fault. It takes two to tango."
- **It's not rocket science** – said about a relatively easy or simple task.
- "You just have to water the flowers occasionally. It's not rocket science."
- **Jump the gun** – to rush or do something too early.
- "I just couldn't wait! I jumped the gun and asked her to marry me last night."
- **Jump to a conclusion** – to make a judgment without hearing all of the evidence.
- "She thinks I'm rich because she saw me wearing a suit and driving a nice rental car. If she saw what I normally drive, she wouldn't have jumped to that conclusion."
- **Just kidding** – something said to indicate that the previous statement was not true and was meant as a joke.
- "She told me that she broke my phone, but then pulled it out and said 'just kidding!'"
- **Kill two birds with one stone** – to take care of two or more problems with one solution.
- "We need to get a new phone and clothes, so let's just go to the mall later and kill two birds with one stone."
- **Let someone off the hook** – to no longer hold someone to doing something they had agreed to.
- "My flight got cancelled, so you are off the hook for taking me to the airport."
- **Make a long story short** – to shorten or skip telling a story to reach the main point.
- "To make a long story short, we had a really good time in our trip to London."
- **No pain, no gain** – said to indicate that doing something can be hard or even painful, but that it indicates progress.
- "Running is so hard, but I have to do it. No pain, no gain."
- **On the ball** – to be ready or aware of what is happening.
- "He always has the reading done ahead of the time. He's really on the ball."
- **Pull someone's leg** – used to indicate joking.
- "I was pulling Susan's leg when I said I won the lottery."
- **Pull yourself together** – said to someone who is visibly emotional in an embarrassing way.

- "You look like an emotional wreck! Pull yourself together."
- **Quick study** – used to describe someone who learns quickly.
- "Everything comes so easily to Jim. He is such a quick study."
- **Rain or shine** – used to indicate that an event will happen no matter what happens. This does not necessarily apply to weather.
- "We are going to watch that new movie on Friday, rain or shine!"
- **Rub the wrong way** – used to indicate that an action or person is irritating.
- "He never seems like he is telling the truth and it really rubs me the wrong way."
- **So far, so good** – the work done up until this point has been done well.
- "I'm halfway done with building my house and so far, so good."
- **Speak of the devil** – said when talking about a person and they show up. Can be positive or negative.
- "Jim is such a nice guy!" (Jim then walks in) "Speak of the devil."
- **That's the last straw** – used to indicate that one too many bad things have happened.
- "My boyfriend spilled coffee on me and constantly says mean things. The last straw, though, was when he broke my phone! I'm going to break up with him."
- **The best of both worlds** – to have the benefits of two situations that usually don't co-exist.
- "She lives far enough away from the city that she can see the stars, but close enough to have a short commute. She really has the best of both worlds."
- **Time flies when you're having fun** – said when time seems to be going faster than normal while enjoying oneself.
- "Our day at the theme park went by too quickly! Time flies when you're having fun."
- **To make matters worse** – usually used last in a list of bad experiences.
- "I had a bad day. I stepped on a nail, ran out of gas, and to make matters worse, I still have to work tonight."
- **Under the weather** – used to say that someone is sick.
- "I can't come to the party tonight; I'm under the weather. "
- **Vice versa** – used to indicate a reversal of two things in the previous statement.
- "You earn money and then you can spend it, not vice versa."
- **We'll cross that bridge when we come to it** – putting off an issue for later.
- "We somehow got the car to start this time, but we will have to fix it at some point. We will cross that bridge when we come to it."
- **Wrap your head around something** – to try to understand.
- "Hey Jim, can you come and look at this?"
- "Not right now, I'm trying to wrap my head around something."
- **You can say that again** – a statement used to indicate agreement to someone else's statement.
- "I can't wait for payday."
- "You can say that again!"
- **Your guess is as good as mine** – used to indicate a lack of knowledge.
- "Hey, do you know which way it is to Peter's house?"
- "Your guess is as good as mine!"
- **Zip your lip** – said to tell someone to be quiet.
- "Hey! Zip your lip, the professor is talking."

# How to Overcome Test Anxiety

Just the thought of taking a test is enough to make most people a little nervous. A test is an important event that can have a long-term impact on your future, so it's important to take it seriously and it's natural to feel anxious about performing well. But just because anxiety is normal, that doesn't mean that it's helpful in test taking, or that you should simply accept it as part of your life. Anxiety can have a variety of effects. These effects can be mild, like making you feel slightly nervous, or severe, like blocking your ability to focus or remember even a simple detail.

If you experience test anxiety—whether severe or mild—it's important to know how to beat it. To discover this, first you need to understand what causes test anxiety.

## Causes of Test Anxiety

While we often think of anxiety as an uncontrollable emotional state, it can actually be caused by simple, practical things. One of the most common causes of test anxiety is that a person does not feel adequately prepared for their test. This feeling can be the result of many different issues such as poor study habits or lack of organization, but the most common culprit is time management. Starting to study too late, failing to organize your study time to cover all of the material, or being distracted while you study will mean that you're not well prepared for the test. This may lead to cramming the night before, which will cause you to be physically and mentally exhausted for the test. Poor time management also contributes to feelings of stress, fear, and hopelessness as you realize you are not well prepared but don't know what to do about it.

Other times, test anxiety is not related to your preparation for the test but comes from unresolved fear. This may be a past failure on a test, or poor performance on tests in general. It may come from comparing yourself to others who seem to be performing better or from the stress of living up to expectations. Anxiety may be driven by fears of the future—how failure on this test would affect your educational and career goals. These fears are often completely irrational, but they can still negatively impact your test performance.

> **Review Video: 3 Reasons You Have Test Anxiety**
> Visit mometrix.com/academy and enter code: 428468

# Elements of Test Anxiety

As mentioned earlier, test anxiety is considered to be an emotional state, but it has physical and mental components as well. Sometimes you may not even realize that you are suffering from test anxiety until you notice the physical symptoms. These can include trembling hands, rapid heartbeat, sweating, nausea, and tense muscles. Extreme anxiety may lead to fainting or vomiting. Obviously, any of these symptoms can have a negative impact on testing. It is important to recognize them as soon as they begin to occur so that you can address the problem before it damages your performance.

> **Review Video: 3 Ways to Tell You Have Test Anxiety**
> Visit mometrix.com/academy and enter code: 927847

The mental components of test anxiety include trouble focusing and inability to remember learned information. During a test, your mind is on high alert, which can help you recall information and stay focused for an extended period of time. However, anxiety interferes with your mind's natural processes, causing you to blank out, even on the questions you know well. The strain of testing during anxiety makes it difficult to stay focused, especially on a test that may take several hours. Extreme anxiety can take a huge mental toll, making it difficult not only to recall test information but even to understand the test questions or pull your thoughts together.

> **Review Video: How Test Anxiety Affects Memory**
> Visit mometrix.com/academy and enter code: 609003

# Effects of Test Anxiety

Test anxiety is like a disease—if left untreated, it will get progressively worse. Anxiety leads to poor performance, and this reinforces the feelings of fear and failure, which in turn lead to poor performances on subsequent tests. It can grow from a mild nervousness to a crippling condition. If allowed to progress, test anxiety can have a big impact on your schooling, and consequently on your future.

Test anxiety can spread to other parts of your life. Anxiety on tests can become anxiety in any stressful situation, and blanking on a test can turn into panicking in a job situation. But fortunately, you don't have to let anxiety rule your testing and determine your grades. There are a number of relatively simple steps you can take to move past anxiety and function normally on a test and in the rest of life.

> **Review Video: How Test Anxiety Impacts Your Grades**
> Visit mometrix.com/academy and enter code: 939819

# Physical Steps for Beating Test Anxiety

While test anxiety is a serious problem, the good news is that it can be overcome. It doesn't have to control your ability to think and remember information. While it may take time, you can begin taking steps today to beat anxiety.

Just as your first hint that you may be struggling with anxiety comes from the physical symptoms, the first step to treating it is also physical. Rest is crucial for having a clear, strong mind. If you are tired, it is much easier to give in to anxiety. But if you establish good sleep habits, your body and mind will be ready to perform optimally, without the strain of exhaustion. Additionally, sleeping well helps you to retain information better, so you're more likely to recall the answers when you see the test questions.

Getting good sleep means more than going to bed on time. It's important to allow your brain time to relax. Take study breaks from time to time so it doesn't get overworked, and don't study right before bed. Take time to rest your mind before trying to rest your body, or you may find it difficult to fall asleep.

> **Review Video: The Importance of Sleep for Your Brain**
> Visit mometrix.com/academy and enter code: 319338

Along with sleep, other aspects of physical health are important in preparing for a test. Good nutrition is vital for good brain function. Sugary foods and drinks may give a burst of energy but this burst is followed by a crash, both physically and emotionally. Instead, fuel your body with protein and vitamin-rich foods.

Also, drink plenty of water. Dehydration can lead to headaches and exhaustion, especially if your brain is already under stress from the rigors of the test. Particularly if your test is a long one, drink water during the breaks. And if possible, take an energy-boosting snack to eat between sections.

> **Review Video: How Diet Can Affect your Mood**
> Visit mometrix.com/academy and enter code: 624317

Along with sleep and diet, a third important part of physical health is exercise. Maintaining a steady workout schedule is helpful, but even taking 5-minute study breaks to walk can help get your blood pumping faster and clear your head. Exercise also releases endorphins, which contribute to a positive feeling and can help combat test anxiety.

When you nurture your physical health, you are also contributing to your mental health. If your body is healthy, your mind is much more likely to be healthy as well. So take time to rest, nourish your body with healthy food and water, and get moving as much as possible. Taking these physical steps will make you stronger and more able to take the mental steps necessary to overcome test anxiety.

> **Review Video: How to Stay Healthy and Prevent Test Anxiety**
> Visit mometrix.com/academy and enter code: 877894

# Mental Steps for Beating Test Anxiety

Working on the mental side of test anxiety can be more challenging, but as with the physical side, there are clear steps you can take to overcome it. As mentioned earlier, test anxiety often stems from lack of preparation, so the obvious solution is to prepare for the test. Effective studying may be the most important weapon you have for beating test anxiety, but you can and should employ several other mental tools to combat fear.

First, boost your confidence by reminding yourself of past success—tests or projects that you aced. If you're putting as much effort into preparing for this test as you did for those, there's no reason you should expect to fail here. Work hard to prepare; then trust your preparation.

Second, surround yourself with encouraging people. It can be helpful to find a study group, but be sure that the people you're around will encourage a positive attitude. If you spend time with others who are anxious or cynical, this will only contribute to your own anxiety. Look for others who are motivated to study hard from a desire to succeed, not from a fear of failure.

Third, reward yourself. A test is physically and mentally tiring, even without anxiety, and it can be helpful to have something to look forward to. Plan an activity following the test, regardless of the outcome, such as going to a movie or getting ice cream.

When you are taking the test, if you find yourself beginning to feel anxious, remind yourself that you know the material. Visualize successfully completing the test. Then take a few deep, relaxing breaths and return to it. Work through the questions carefully but with confidence, knowing that you are capable of succeeding.

Developing a healthy mental approach to test taking will also aid in other areas of life. Test anxiety affects more than just the actual test—it can be damaging to your mental health and even contribute to depression. It's important to beat test anxiety before it becomes a problem for more than testing.

**Review Video: Test Anxiety and Depression**
Visit mometrix.com/academy and enter code: 904704

# Study Strategy

Being prepared for the test is necessary to combat anxiety, but what does being prepared look like? You may study for hours on end and still not feel prepared. What you need is a strategy for test prep. The next few pages outline our recommended steps to help you plan out and conquer the challenge of preparation.

## STEP 1: SCOPE OUT THE TEST

Learn everything you can about the format (multiple choice, essay, etc.) and what will be on the test. Gather any study materials, course outlines, or sample exams that may be available. Not only will this help you to prepare, but knowing what to expect can help to alleviate test anxiety.

## STEP 2: MAP OUT THE MATERIAL

Look through the textbook or study guide and make note of how many chapters or sections it has. Then divide these over the time you have. For example, if a book has 15 chapters and you have five days to study, you need to cover three chapters each day. Even better, if you have the time, leave an extra day at the end for overall review after you have gone through the material in depth.

If time is limited, you may need to prioritize the material. Look through it and make note of which sections you think you already have a good grasp on, and which need review. While you are studying, skim quickly through the familiar sections and take more time on the challenging parts. Write out your plan so you don't get lost as you go. Having a written plan also helps you feel more in control of the study, so anxiety is less likely to arise from feeling overwhelmed at the amount to cover.

## STEP 3: GATHER YOUR TOOLS

Decide what study method works best for you. Do you prefer to highlight in the book as you study and then go back over the highlighted portions? Or do you type out notes of the important information? Or is it helpful to make flashcards that you can carry with you? Assemble the pens, index cards, highlighters, post-it notes, and any other materials you may need so you won't be distracted by getting up to find things while you study.

If you're having a hard time retaining the information or organizing your notes, experiment with different methods. For example, try color-coding by subject with colored pens, highlighters, or post-it notes. If you learn better by hearing, try recording yourself reading your notes so you can listen while in the car, working out, or simply sitting at your desk. Ask a friend to quiz you from your flashcards, or try teaching someone the material to solidify it in your mind.

## STEP 4: CREATE YOUR ENVIRONMENT

It's important to avoid distractions while you study. This includes both the obvious distractions like visitors and the subtle distractions like an uncomfortable chair (or a too-comfortable couch that makes you want to fall asleep). Set up the best study environment possible: good lighting and a comfortable work area. If background music helps you focus, you may want to turn it on, but otherwise keep the room quiet. If you are using a computer to take notes, be sure you don't have any other windows open, especially applications like social media, games, or anything else that could distract you. Silence your phone and turn off notifications. Be sure to keep water close by so you stay hydrated while you study (but avoid unhealthy drinks and snacks).

Also, take into account the best time of day to study. Are you freshest first thing in the morning? Try to set aside some time then to work through the material. Is your mind clearer in the afternoon or evening? Schedule your study session then. Another method is to study at the same time of day that you will take the test, so that your brain gets used to working on the material at that time and will be ready to focus at test time.

## STEP 5: STUDY!

Once you have done all the study preparation, it's time to settle into the actual studying. Sit down, take a few moments to settle your mind so you can focus, and begin to follow your study plan. Don't give in to distractions or let yourself procrastinate. This is your time to prepare so you'll be ready to fearlessly approach the test. Make the most of the time and stay focused.

Of course, you don't want to burn out. If you study too long you may find that you're not retaining the information very well. Take regular study breaks. For example, taking five minutes out of every hour to walk briskly, breathing deeply and swinging your arms, can help your mind stay fresh.

As you get to the end of each chapter or section, it's a good idea to do a quick review. Remind yourself of what you learned and work on any difficult parts. When you feel that you've mastered the material, move on to the next part. At the end of your study session, briefly skim through your notes again.

But while review is helpful, cramming last minute is NOT. If at all possible, work ahead so that you won't need to fit all your study into the last day. Cramming overloads your brain with more information than it can process and retain, and your tired mind may struggle to recall even previously learned information when it is overwhelmed with last-minute study. Also, the urgent nature of cramming and the stress placed on your brain contribute to anxiety. You'll be more likely to go to the test feeling unprepared and having trouble thinking clearly.

So don't cram, and don't stay up late before the test, even just to review your notes at a leisurely pace. Your brain needs rest more than it needs to go over the information again. In fact, plan to finish your studies by noon or early afternoon the day before the test. Give your brain the rest of the day to relax or focus on other things, and get a good night's sleep. Then you will be fresh for the test and better able to recall what you've studied.

## STEP 6: TAKE A PRACTICE TEST

Many courses offer sample tests, either online or in the study materials. This is an excellent resource to check whether you have mastered the material, as well as to prepare for the test format and environment.

Check the test format ahead of time: the number of questions, the type (multiple choice, free response, etc.), and the time limit. Then create a plan for working through them. For example, if you have 30 minutes to take a 60-question test, your limit is 30 seconds per question. Spend less time on the questions you know well so that you can take more time on the difficult ones.

If you have time to take several practice tests, take the first one open book, with no time limit. Work through the questions at your own pace and make sure you fully understand them. Gradually work up to taking a test under test conditions: sit at a desk with all study materials put away and set a timer. Pace yourself to make sure you finish the test with time to spare and go back to check your answers if you have time.

After each test, check your answers. On the questions you missed, be sure you understand why you missed them. Did you misread the question (tests can use tricky wording)? Did you forget the information? Or was it something you hadn't learned? Go back and study any shaky areas that the practice tests reveal.

Taking these tests not only helps with your grade, but also aids in combating test anxiety. If you're already used to the test conditions, you're less likely to worry about it, and working through tests until you're scoring well gives you a confidence boost. Go through the practice tests until you feel comfortable, and then you can go into the test knowing that you're ready for it.

## Test Tips

On test day, you should be confident, knowing that you've prepared well and are ready to answer the questions. But aside from preparation, there are several test day strategies you can employ to maximize your performance.

First, as stated before, get a good night's sleep the night before the test (and for several nights before that, if possible). Go into the test with a fresh, alert mind rather than staying up late to study.

Try not to change too much about your normal routine on the day of the test. It's important to eat a nutritious breakfast, but if you normally don't eat breakfast at all, consider eating just a protein bar. If you're a coffee drinker, go ahead and have your normal coffee. Just make sure you time it so that the caffeine doesn't wear off right in the middle of your test. Avoid sugary beverages, and drink enough water to stay hydrated but not so much that you need a restroom break 10 minutes into the test. If your test isn't first thing in the morning, consider going for a walk or doing a light workout before the test to get your blood flowing.

Allow yourself enough time to get ready, and leave for the test with plenty of time to spare so you won't have the anxiety of scrambling to arrive in time. Another reason to be early is to select a good seat. It's helpful to sit away from doors and windows, which can be distracting. Find a good seat, get out your supplies, and settle your mind before the test begins.

When the test begins, start by going over the instructions carefully, even if you already know what to expect. Make sure you avoid any careless mistakes by following the directions.

Then begin working through the questions, pacing yourself as you've practiced. If you're not sure on an answer, don't spend too much time on it, and don't let it shake your confidence. Either skip it and come back later, or eliminate as many wrong answers as possible and guess among the remaining ones. Don't dwell on these questions as you continue—put them out of your mind and focus on what lies ahead.

Be sure to read all of the answer choices, even if you're sure the first one is the right answer. Sometimes you'll find a better one if you keep reading. But don't second-guess yourself if you do immediately know the answer. Your gut instinct is usually right. Don't let test anxiety rob you of the information you know.

If you have time at the end of the test (and if the test format allows), go back and review your answers. Be cautious about changing any, since your first instinct tends to be correct, but make sure you didn't misread any of the questions or accidentally mark the wrong answer choice. Look over any you skipped and make an educated guess.

At the end, leave the test feeling confident. You've done your best, so don't waste time worrying about your performance or wishing you could change anything. Instead, celebrate the successful

completion of this test. And finally, use this test to learn how to deal with anxiety even better next time.

## Important Qualification

Not all anxiety is created equal. If your test anxiety is causing major issues in your life beyond the classroom or testing center, or if you are experiencing troubling physical symptoms related to your anxiety, it may be a sign of a serious physiological or psychological condition. If this sounds like your situation, we strongly encourage you to seek professional help.

# Thank You

We at Mometrix would like to extend our heartfelt thanks to you, our friend and patron, for allowing us to play a part in your journey. It is a privilege to serve people from all walks of life who are unified in their commitment to building the best future they can for themselves.

The preparation you devote to these important testing milestones may be the most valuable educational opportunity you have for making a real difference in your life. We encourage you to put your heart into it—that feeling of succeeding, overcoming, and yes, conquering will be well worth the hours you've invested.

We want to hear your story, your struggles and your successes, and if you see any opportunities for us to improve our materials so we can help others even more effectively in the future, please share that with us as well. **The team at Mometrix would be absolutely thrilled to hear from you!** So please, send us an email (support@mometrix.com) and let's stay in touch.

> **If you'd like some additional help, check out these other resources we offer for your exam:**
> http://mometrixflashcards.com/TOEFL

# Additional Bonus Material

Due to our efforts to try to keep this book to a manageable length, we've created a link that will give you access to all of your additional bonus material.

**Please visit http://www.mometrix.com/bonus948/toefl to access the information.**

114